# Journey with the
# FATHERS

# The Word of God Throughout the Ages

## New Testament

**2**

# F Journey with the ATHERS

*Commentaries on the Sunday Gospels*

## Year B

*edited by*
Edith Barnecut, O.S.B.

*foreword by*
John E. Rotelle, O.S.A.

New City Press

Published in the United States by New City Press
202 Cardinal Rd., Hyde Park, NY 12538
©1993 New City Press

Readings and biographical sketches
©1981, 1984 Friends of Henry Ashworth.

Excerpts from Catherine of Siena, *The Dialogue*, trans. by Suzanne Noffke,
and Catherine of Genoa, *Purgation and Purgatory*, trans. by Serge Hughes
©1980 and 1979 Missionary Society of St. Paul the Apostle.
Used by permission of Paulist Press.

Library of Congress Cataloging-in-Publication Data:

Journey with the Fathers

   (the word of God throughout the ages.　New Testament)
   Includes bibliographical references and indexes.
   Contents: [1] Year A — [2] Year B.
   1. Bible. N.T. Gospels—Commentaries　2. Church
year—Orater-books and devotions—English.　3. Fathers
of the church.　　I. Barnecut, Edith.
   BX2178.J68　　1992　　264'.34　　　　　　　　　　92-20685
   ISBN 1-56548-013-9 (v. 1)
   ISBN 1-56548-056-2 (v. 2)

1st printing: September 1993
2d printing: July 1995

Printed in the United States of America

# Contents

## Editor's Note

This collection of homilies on the Sunday gospels and principal feasts which replace the Sunday celebration is largely a revision of that first published for the Benedictine Office of Vigils. Texts drawn from the patristic period, supplemented by some from later writers following the same tradition, are now offered to a wider public in a fresh format.

# *Foreword*

Throughout the Christian centuries the Bible, especially the gospels, has inspired many volumes of sermons and commentaries. Those written in the early ages of the Church have a special value because of their formative influence on later theology and spirituality—the two were always wedded. It was for this reason that some of the early Christian writers came to be known as the "Fathers of the Church."

The esteem in which these early writings were held is shown by the great labor that was undertaken to copy them by hand so that they became familiar to scholars throughout the known world. Sermons preached by Saint Augustine of Hippo in North Africa in the fifth century were read by Saint Bede in England in the eighth.

Meanwhile translations were being made, though these were mostly of the theological and philosophical works of the Fathers or Church writers, the sermons receiving less attention. Not all of these writings, even of the sermons, speak to people of our day. Many are too diffuse for modern taste, or deal with subjects which are no longer of current interest. To find the gems concealed in this huge mass of material requires great labor, but this was undertaken after the Second Vatican Council to produce the readings in the revised Liturgy of the Hours published in 1970 and later translated into the various languages. This put the choicest passages from our patristic heritage within reach of the general reader. It was quickly supplemented by other collections of patristic and modern readings, one such being the present series *Journey with the Fathers* which will deepen one's understanding of the gospels read at Mass on Sundays or feasts which replace a Sunday. It puts within reach of all some of the treasures of our Christian tradition.

*John E. Rotelle, O.S.A.*

# First Sunday of Advent

*Gospel:* Mark 13:33-37

Stay awake! You never know when the Lord will come.

*Commentary:* Augustine

*Our God will come openly; our God will come and will not keep silent.* The first coming of Christ the Lord, God's Son and our God, was in obscurity; the second will be in sight of the whole world. When he came in obscurity no one recognized him but his own servants; when he comes openly he will be known by both good people and bad. When he came in obscurity, it was to be judged; when he comes openly it will be to judge. He was silent at his trial, as the prophet foretold: *He was like a sheep led to the slaughter, like a lamb before his shearers. He did not open his mouth.* But, *Our God will come openly; our God will come and will not keep silence.* Silent when accused, he will not be silent as judge. And he is not silent now. By no means; when people of today recognize his voice and despise him, Scripture assures us that he will not be silent, he will not hold his hand.

Nowadays when the divine commands are spoken of, some people begin to jeer. They are not at present shown what God promises, they do not see what he threatens—so they laugh at his commands. After all, good people and bad enjoy this world's so-called happiness; good people and bad suffer from what are deemed this world's misfortunes. Those whose lives are geared to the present rather than the future are impressed by the fact that this world's blessings and sufferings fall to the lot of good and bad without distinction. If wealth is their ambition, they see it being enjoyed not only by decent folk, but also by people of the worst kind. If they are in dread of poverty and all the other miseries of this world, they also see that the good and the bad both suffer from them. Therefore they say to themselves, "God does not care about human affairs, he exercises no control over them. On the

**Thank you for choosing this book.
If you would like to receive regular information
about New City Press titles, please fill in this card.**

Title purchased: _____

_____

**Please check the subjects
that are of particular interest to you:**

- [ ] **FATHERS OF THE CHURCH**

- [ ] **CLASSICS IN SPIRITUALITY**

- [ ] **CONTEMPORARY SPIRITUALITY**

- [ ] **THEOLOGY**

- [ ] **SCRIPTURE AND COMMENTARIES**

- [ ] **FAMILY LIFE**

- [ ] **BIOGRAPHY / HISTORY**

Other subjects of interest: _____

_____

Name: _____

Address: _____

_____

**NEW CITY PRESS**
202 CARDINAL RD.
HYDE PARK NY 12538

contrary; he has sent us into the abyss of this world, and simply abandoned us to its sufferings. He shows no sign of his providence." Consequently, seeing no evidence of anyone being called to account, such people hold God's commands in derision.

Nevertheless, each person would do well to take thought even now, because when he wills to do so, God looks, and he judges; he will not tolerate an hour's delay. When he wills to do so, he waits. Why does he do this? Surely if he never passed judgment in this present life, some people would think he does not exist. But if he always gave sentence here and now, there would be nothing reserved for the Day of Judgment. That is why much is kept for that day; but in order to put the fear of God into those whose cases are deferred, and so convert them, some judgments are made here and now.

For it is clear that God takes no pleasure in condemning. His desire is to save, and he bears patiently with evil people in order to make them good. Yet we have the Apostle's warning: *The wrath of God will be revealed from heaven against all ungodliness, and God will reward each one according to his deeds.* The Apostle takes scoffers to task by asking them: *Do you think lightly of God's abundant goodness and his forbearance?* Do you despise him and think his judgment a matter of no account because he is good to you, because he is long-suffering and bears with you patiently, because he delays the day of reckoning and does not destroy you out of hand? *Do you not know that the patience of God is meant to lead you to repentance? By the hardness of your heart you are storing up wrath against yourself on that Day of Retribution,* when the righteous judgment of God will be revealed and he will give every one the reward his or her deeds deserve.

*(Sermon 18, 1-2: PL 38, 128-29)*

---

**Augustine** (354-430) was born at Thagaste in Africa and received a Christian education, although he was not baptized until 387. In 391 he was ordained priest and in 395 he became coadjutor bishop to Valerius of Hippo, whom he succeeded in 396. Augustine's theology was formulated in the course of his struggle with three heresies: Manichaeism, Donatism, and Pelagianism. His writings are voluminous and his influence on subsequent theology immense. He molded the thought of the Middle Ages down to the thirteenth century. Yet he was above all a pastor and a great spiritual writer.

# Second Sunday of Advent

*Gospel:* Mark 1:1-8

Prepare a way for the Lord.

*Commentary:* Origen

Let us examine the scriptural texts foretelling the coming of Christ. One such prophecy begins with a reference to John the Baptist: *The voice of one crying in the wilderness, Prepare the way of the Lord; make his paths straight.* What follows, however, applies directly to our Lord and Savior, since it is by Jesus rather than by John that *every valley has been filled in.*

You have only to recall the kind of people you were before you put your faith in the Lord to see yourselves as deep valleys, as pits plunging precipitously into the lowest depths. But now that the Lord Jesus has come and has sent the Holy Spirit in his name, all your valleys have been filled in with good works and the Holy Spirit's fruits. Love no longer tolerates the presence of valleys in your lives; if peace, patience, and goodness find a home in you, not only will each of you cease to be a valley but you will actually begin to be a mountain of God.

Among the pagans we daily see this prophetic filling of every valley realized, just as among the people of Israel, now deprived of their former privileged status, we see the overthrowing of every mountain and hill. But *because of their offense, salvation has come to the pagans, to stir Israel to emulation.*

If you prefer you can visualize these fallen mountains and hills as the hostile powers that formerly raised themselves up in opposition to the human race. Such an interpretation is legitimate because, in order to fill in the kind of valleys we have been speaking of, the enemy powers—the mountains and hills—must be laid low.

Now let us turn to that part of the prophecy which also concerns the

12

coming of Christ and see whether this too has been fulfilled. The text continues: *Every crooked way shall be straightened.* Each one of us was once crooked; if we are no longer so, it is entirely due to the grace of Christ. Through his coming to our souls all our crooked ways have been straightened out. If Christ did not come to your soul, of what use would his historical coming in the flesh be to you? Let us pray that each day we may experience his coming and be able to say: *It is no longer I who live, but Christ who lives in me.*

Jesus my Lord has come, then. He has smoothed out your rough places and changed your disorderly ways into level paths, making in you an even unimpeded road, a road that is absolutely clear, so that God the Father may walk in you and Christ the Lord make his dwelling in you and say: *My Father and I will come and make our home in them.*

*(Homily on Luke's Gospel 22, 1-4: SC 67, 300-02)*

---

**Origen** (183-253), one of the greatest thinkers of ancient times, became head of the catechetical school of Alexandria at the age of eighteen. In 230 he was ordained priest by the bishop of Caesarea. His life was entirely devoted to the study of Scripture and he was also a great master of the spiritual life. His book *On First Principles* was the first great theological synthesis. Many of his works are extant only in Latin as a result of his posthumous condemnation for heterodox teaching. Nevertheless, in intention he was always a loyal son of the Church.

# Third Sunday of Advent

*Gospel:* John 1:6-8.19-28

There stands among you, unknown to you, the one who is coming after me.

*Commentary:* John Scotus Erigena

Into the theological plan of his gospel John the evangelist draws John the Baptist; deep calls to deep at the utterance of divine mysteries. We hear the evangelist relating the story of the forerunner, the man whose gift it was to know the Word as he was in the beginning, speaking to us of the one who was commissioned to go ahead of the Word made flesh. *There was,* says the evangelist, not simply a messenger of God, but *a man.* This he said in order to distinguish the man who shared only the humanity of the one he heralded from the man who came after him, the man who united godhead and manhood in his own person. The evangelist's intention was to differentiate between the fleeting voice and the eternally unchanging Word. The one, he would suggest, was the morning star appearing at the dawning of the kingdom of heaven, while the other was the Sun of Justice coming in its wake. He distinguished the witness from the one to whom he testified, the messenger from him who sent him, the lamp burning in the night from the brilliant light that filled the whole world, the light that dispelled the darkness of death and sin from the entire human race.

So then, the Lord's forerunner was a man, not a god; whereas the Lord whom he preceded was both man and God. The forerunner was a man destined to be divinized by God's grace, whereas the one he preceded was God by nature, who, through his desire to save and redeem us, lowered himself in order to assume our human nature.

A man was sent. By whom? By the divine Word, whose forerunner he was. To go before the Lord was his mission. Lifting up his voice, this man called out: *The voice of one crying in the wilderness!* It was the herald preparing the way for the Lord's coming. John was his name; John to whom was given the grace to go ahead of the King of Kings, to point out to the world the Word made flesh, to baptize him with that baptism in which the Spirit would manifest his divine sonship, to give witness through his teaching and martyrdom to the eternal light.

*(Homily on John's Prologue 15: SC 151:275-77)*

**Erigena, John Scotus** (c. 810-77) received his early education, which included some Greek, in Ireland, the country of his birth. Having won the patronage of Charles the Bald, he became head of the palace school at Laon. He was not a monk, and probably never became a priest. Erigena translated into Latin the works of Pseudo-Denis, the *Ambigua* of Maximus the Confessor, and the *De Hominis Opificio* of Gregory of Nyssa. His greatest work was *De Divisione Naturae* or *Periphyseon.* The first medieval theological synthesis, it shows a strong influence of the Greek theological tradition. Erigena was a profoundly original thinker. His obscure and paradoxical language has at times been misunderstood and led to accusations of heresy, and his Neoplatonism did lead him into error on some points. He was, nevertheless, the greatest theologian of his time in East or West.

# Fourth Sunday of Advent

*Gospel:* Luke 1:26-38

You shall conceive and bear a son.

*Commentary:* Bede

Today's reading of the gospel calls to mind the beginning of our redemption, for the passage tells us how God sent an angel from heaven to a virgin. He was to proclaim the new birth, the incarnation of God's Son, who would take away our age-old guilt; through him it would be possible for us to be made new and numbered among the children of God. And so, if we are to deserve the gifts of the promised salvation, we must listen attentively to the account of its beginning.

*The angel Gabriel was sent from God to a city of Galilee named Nazareth, to a virgin betrothed to a man whose name was Joseph of the house of David; and the virgin's name was Mary.* What is said of the house of David applies not only to Joseph but also to Mary. It was a precept of the law that each man should marry a wife from his own tribe and kindred. Saint Paul also bears testimony to this when he writes to Timothy: *Remember Jesus Christ, risen from the dead, descended from David, as preached in my gospel.* Our Lord is truly descended from David, since his spotless mother took her ancestry from David's line.

*The angel came to her and said, "Do not be afraid, Mary, for you have found favor with God. And behold, you will conceive in your womb and bear a son, and you shall call his name Jesus. He will be great, and will be called the Son of the Most High; and the Lord God will give to him the throne of his father David."* The angel refers to the kingdom of the Israelite nation as the throne of David because in his time, by the Lord's command and assistance, David governed it with a spirit of faithful service. The Lord God gave to our Redeemer the throne of his father David, when he decreed that he should take flesh from the lineage of David. As David had once ruled the people with temporal authority, so Christ would now lead them to the eternal kingdom by his spiritual grace. Of this kingdom the Apostle said: *He has delivered us from the dominion of darkness and transferred us to the kingdom of his beloved Son.*

*He will reign over the house of Jacob for ever.* The house of Jacob here refers to the universal Church which, through its faith in and witness to Christ, shares the heritage of the patriarchs. This may apply either to those who are physical descendants of the patriarchal families, or to those who come from gentile nations and are reborn in Christ by the waters of baptism. In this house Christ shall reign for ever, and *of his kingdom there will be no end.* During this present life, Christ rules in the Church. By faith and love he dwells in the hearts of his elect, and guides them by his unceasing care toward their heavenly reward. In the life to come, when their period of exile on earth is ended, he will exercise his kingship by leading the faithful to their heavenly country. There, for ever inspired by the vision of his presence, their one delight will be to praise and glorify him.

*(Homily 3 on Advent: CCL 122, 14-17)*

---

**Bede** (c. 673-735), who received the title of Venerable less than a century after his death, was placed at the age of seven in the monastery of Wearmouth, then ruled by Saint Benet Biscop. From there he was sent to Jarrow, probably at the time of its foundation in about 681. At the age of thirty he was ordained priest. His whole life was devoted to the study of Scripture, to teaching, writing, and the prayer of the Divine Office. He was famous for his learning, although he never went beyond the bounds of his native Northumbria. Bede is best known for his historical works, which earned him the title "Father of English History." His *Historia Ecclesiastica Gentis Anglorum* is a primary source for early English history, especially valuable because of the care he took to give his authorities, and to separate historical fact from hearsay and tradition. In 1899 Bede was proclaimed a doctor of the Church.

# Christmas

*Gospel:* Luke 2:1-14

Today a Savior has been born for you.

*Commentary:* Aelred

*Today, in the city of David, the Savior of the world is born for us: he is Christ the Lord.* That city is Bethlehem. We must run there as the shepherds did when they heard these tidings, and so put into action the words we traditionally sing at this season: *They sang of God's glory, they hastened to Bethlehem.*

And this shall be a sign for you: you will find the child wrapped in swaddling bands and lying in a manger. Now this is what I say: you must love. You fear the Lord of angels, yes, but love the tiny babe; you fear the Lord of majesty, yes, but love the infant wrapped in swaddling clothes; you fear him who reigns in heaven, yes, but love him who lies in the manger.

What sort of sign were the shepherds given? You will find the child wrapped in swaddling clothes and lying in a manger. It was by this that they were to recognize their Savior and Lord. But is there anything great about being wrapped in swaddling clothes and lying in a stable— are not other children also wrapped in swaddling clothes? What kind of sign, then, can this be?

Indeed it is a great one, if only we understand it rightly. Such understanding will be ours if this message of love is not restricted to our hearing, but if our hearts too are illuminated by the light which accompanied the appearance of the angels. The angel who first proclaimed the good tidings appeared surrounded by light to teach us that only those whose minds are spiritually enlightened can truly understand the message.

Much can be said of this sign; but as time is passing, I shall say little, and briefly. Bethlehem, the house of bread, is holy Church, in which is distributed the body of Christ, the true bread. The manger at Bethlehem is the altar of the church; it is there that Christ's creatures are fed. This is the table of which it is written, You have prepared a banquet for me. In this manger is Jesus, wrapped in the swaddling clothes which are the outward form of the sacraments. Here in this manger, under the species of bread and wine, is the true body and blood of Christ. We believe that Christ himself is here, but he is wrapped in swaddling clothes; in other words, he is invisibly contained in these sacraments. We have no greater or clearer proof of Christ's birth than our daily reception of his body and blood at the holy altar, and the sight of him who was once born for us of a virgin daily offered in sacrifice for us.

And so let us hasten to the manger of the Lord. But before drawing near we must prepare ourselves as well as we can with the help of his grace; and then, in company with the angels, with pure heart, good conscience, and unfeigned faith, we may sing to the Lord in all that we do throughout the whole of our life: *Glory to God in the highest, and peace to his people on earth;* through our Lord Jesus Christ, to whom be honor and glory for ever and ever. Amen.

*(Sermon 2 on Christmas: PL 195, 226-27)*

---

**Aelred of Rievaulx** (1109-67), a native of Yorkshire, spent part of his youth at the court of King David of Scotland. About the year 1133 he entered the Cistercian monastery of Rievaulx of which he later became abbot. His writings, which combine mystical and speculative theology, earned him the title, "The Bernard of the North." The most important works of this master of the spiritual life are *The Mirror of Charity* and *Spiritual Friendship.*

# Holy Family

*Gospel:* Luke 2:22-40 or 39-40

The child grew to maturity, and he was filled with wisdom.

*Commentary:* Cyril of Alexandria

We see Emmanuel as a newborn infant lying in a manger. In his human condition he is wrapped in swaddling clothes, but in his divine nature he is hymned by angels. Angels brought the shepherds the good news of his birth, for God the Father had given those who dwell in heaven the special privilege of being his first heralds.

Today we also see him submitting to the law of Moses; or rather, we see God the lawgiver subject as man to his own decrees. The reason for this we learn from the wisdom of Paul. He says: *When we were under age we were slaves of the elemental spirits of the universe, but when the fullness of time had come God sent his Son, born of a woman, born under the law, to redeem those who were under the law.*

Christ ransomed from the law's curse those who were subject to the law but had never kept it. How did he ransom them? By fulfilling the law. Or to put it in another way, to blot out the reproach of Adam's transgression, he offered himself on our behalf to God the Father, showing him in all things ready obedience and submission. Scripture says: *As through one man's disobedience many were made sinners, so through one man's obedience many will be made righteous.* And so, Christ submitted to the law together with us, and he did so by becoming man in accordance with the divine dispensation.

It was fitting that Christ should do everything that justice required. He had in all truth assumed the condition of a slave; and so, reckoned among those under the yoke by reason of his humanity, he once paid the half-shekel to those who demanded it, although as the Son he was by nature free and not liable to this tax. When you see him keeping the law, then, do not misunderstand it, or reduce one who is free to the rank of household slaves, but reflect rather on the depths of God's plan.

When the eighth day arrived on which it was customary for the flesh to be circumcised as prescribed by the law, he received the name, Jesus, which means "salvation of the people"; for it was the wish of God the Father that his own Son, born of a woman, should be so named. It was then that he first became the salvation of the people and not of one people only but of many, indeed of all peoples and of the whole world.

Christ thus became the light of revelation to the Gentiles, but he is also the glory of Israel. Even though some members of that race were insolent and unbelieving, a remnant has been saved and glorified by Christ. The holy disciples were the firstfruits of Israel, and the brightness of their glory illuminates the whole world. Christ is the glory of Israel in another way too, for in his human nature he came from that people, even though he is God, sovereign ruler of all and blessed for ever.

The wise evangelist helps us, then, by teaching us all the Son of God made flesh endured for our sake and in our name, and that he did not disdain to take upon himself our poverty, so that we might glorify him as Redeemer, as Lord, as Savior, and as God; for to him, and with him to God the Father and the Holy Spirit, belong glory and power for endless ages. Amen.

*(Homily 12: PG 77, 1042.1046.1047.1050)*

---

**Cyril of Alexandria** (d. 444) succeeded his uncle Theophilus as patriarch in 412. Until 428 the pen of this brilliant theologian was employed in exegesis and polemics against the Arians; after that date it was devoted almost entirely to refuting the Nestorian heresy. The teaching of Nestorius was condemned in 431 by the Council of Ephesus at which Cyril presided, and Mary's title, Mother of God, was solemnly recognized. The incarnation is central to Cyril's theology. Only if Christ is consubstantial with the Father and with us can he save us, for the meeting ground between God and ourselves is the flesh of Christ. Through our kinship with Christ, the Word made flesh, we become children of God, and share in the filial relation of the Son with the Father.

# Mary, Mother of God

*Gospel:* Luke 2:16-21

The shepherds found Mary and Joseph and the child.

*Commentary:* John Chrysostom

May we all receive the benefit of having recourse to the holy Virgin and Mother of God. Those of you who are now virgins should be devoted to the mother of the Lord, because it is she who procures for you this fair and incorruptible possession. Truly great is the wonder of the Virgin. What can ever be found greater than all that exists? She alone has appeared wider than earth and heaven. Who is holier than she? She is unsurpassed by our ancestors, by the prophets, apostles, or martyrs, by the patriarchs or the Fathers, by the angels, thrones, dominions, seraphim or cherubim, or by any other created thing visible or invisible. She is a servant and the Mother of God, a virgin and a mother. And let no one be doubtful and ask how she can be a servant and the Mother of God, or how she can be a virgin and a mother. Accept with faith and do not doubt teachings that have been examined and approved by the Fathers. Instead, stand in awe and believe without question, or rather, without being inquisitive. If your beliefs correspond to your own ideas, perceive your danger. But if you believe the word that is preached, it is no longer you who must render an account but the bishop.

Believe what we say about the Virgin, then, and do not hesitate to confess her to be both servant and Mother of God, both virgin and mother. She is a servant as the creature of him who was born of her; she is the Mother of God inasmuch as of her God was born in human flesh. She is a virgin because she did not conceive from the seed of man; she is a mother because she gave birth and became the mother of him who before all eternity was begotten of the Father.

She is therefore the mother of the Lord of angels and our mother;

from her the Son of God received the human body in which he consented to be crucified. Do you desire to know how far the Virgin surpasses the powers of heaven? Give me your attention then. They veil their faces as they hover in fear and trembling, but she offers the human race to God, and through her we receive the forgiveness of our sins. She bore him whom the angels glorified when they came with reverence to be present at his birth. *Glory to God in the highest,* they sang, *and peace to his people on earth.*

Rejoice then, mother and heaven, maiden and cloud, virgin and throne, the boast and foundation of our Church. Plead earnestly for us that through you we may obtain mercy on the Day of Judgment and attain the good things reserved for those who love God, through the grace and love of our Lord Jesus Christ, to whom with the Father and the Holy Spirit be glory, power, and honor now and for ever and for all eternity. Amen

*(Homily attributed to John Chrysostom: Orientalia
Christiana Periodica, 32, 1966)*

---

**John Chrysostom** (c. 347-407) was born at Antioch and studied under Diodore of Tarsus, the leader of the Antiochene school of theology. After a period of great austerity as a hermit, he returned to Antioch where he was ordained deacon in 381 and priest in 386. From 386 to 397 it was his duty to preach in the principal church of the city, and his best homilies, which earned him the title "Chrysostomos" or "the golden-mouthed," were preached at this time. In 397 Chrysostom became patriarch of Constantinople, where his efforts to reform the court, clergy, and people led to his exile in 404 and finally to his death from the hardships imposed on him. Chrysostom stressed the divinity of Christ against the Arians and his full humanity against the Apollinarians, but he had no speculative bent. He was above all a pastor of souls, and was one of the most attractive personalities of the early Church.

# Second Sunday after Christmas

*Gospel:* John 1:1-8 or 1-5.9-14

The Word was made flesh and lived among us.

*Commentary:* Guerric of Igny

You have assembled here to listen to the Word of God, but God has provided something better. Today it is given us not only to hear the Word of God, but even to see it, if only we will *go over to Bethlehem and see this Word which the Lord has brought to pass and shown to us.*

God knew that human perceptions could not reach to things invisible. Human beings were incapable of learning heavenly teaching, finding it difficult to believe anything not brought visibly before their senses. The fact of the matter is that although faith comes by hearing, it comes much more readily and quickly by sight. We learn this from the example of the apostle to whom it was said: "You believe because you have seen me; as long as you only had the evidence of your ears, you remained in unbelief."

But God desires to accommodate himself to our slowness in every way, and therefore his Word, which formerly he had made audible, he has today made visible and even tangible. For this reason people of flesh and blood like ourselves have been able to talk of *that which was from the beginning, which we have seen with our eyes, which we have looked upon and touched with our hands.* They could speak of the Word of Life.

From the beginning the Word was of that eternity which had no beginning; we have heard him promised from the beginning of time; we have seen and touched with our hands the one who is now shown to us at the end of time. Sometimes I have noticed that God's words arouse no interest when they are merely heard with the ears, but if anyone actually saw the Word which is God, how could he fail to rejoice? I will pass judgment on myself in the first place. The Word which is God offers himself to me today to be seen in my own nature; if this does not fill me with joy, then I am an unbeliever. If it does not instruct me, I am a castaway.

If anyone here finds it tedious to listen to this second-rate sermon, far be it from me to weary him with my poor words. Let him go over to Bethlehem, and there let him contemplate that Word on which the angels desire to gaze, the Word of God which the Lord has shown to us. Let him picture in his heart what the living and active Word of God was like as he lay there in the manger.

This is a faithful saying and worthy to be received: your almighty Word, O Lord, which made its way down in deep silence from the Father's royal throne into the cattle stall, speaks to us the better for its silence.

*(Sermon 5 on Christmas, 1-2: SC 166, 223-26)*

---

**Guerric of Igny** (c. 1070/80-1157), about whose early life little is known, probably received his education at the cathedral school of Tournai, perhaps under the influence of Odo of Cambrai (1087-92). He seems to have lived a retired life of prayer and study near the cathedral of Tournai. He paid a visit to Clairvaux to consult Saint Bernard, and is mentioned by him as a novice in a letter to Ogerius in 1125/26. He became abbot of the Cistercian abbey of Igny, in the diocese of Rheims in 1138. A collection of fifty-four authentic sermons preached on Sundays and feast days have been edited. Guerric's spirituality was influenced by Origen.

# *Epiphany*

*Gospel:* Matthew 2:1-12

We have come from the East to worship the king.

*Commentary:* Leo the Great

Dearly beloved, the day on which Christ first showed himself to the Gentiles as the Savior of the world should be held in holy reverence among us. We should experience in our hearts the same joy as the three wise men felt when the sign of the new star led them into the presence of the king of heaven and earth, and they gazed in adoration upon the one in whose promised coming they had put their faith. Although that day belongs to the past, the power of the mystery which was then revealed has not passed away; we are not left with a mere report of bygone events, to be received in faith and remembered with veneration. God's bounty toward us has been multiplied, so that even in our own times we daily experience the grace which belonged to those first beginnings.

The gospel story specifically recalls the days when, without any previous teaching from the prophets or instruction in the law, three men came from the far east in search of God; but we see the same thing taking place even more clearly and extensively in the enlightenment of all those whom God calls at the present time. We see the fulfillment of that prophecy of Isaiah which says: *The Lord has bared his holy arm in the sight of all nations, and the whole world has seen the salvation that comes from the Lord our God.* And again: *Those who have not been told about him shall see, and those who have not heard shall understand.* When we see people being led out of the abyss of error and called to knowledge of the true light, people who, far from professing faith in Jesus Christ, have hitherto devoted themselves to worldly wisdom, we can have no doubt that the splendor of divine grace is at work. Whenever a shaft of light newly pierces darkened

26

hearts, its source is the radiance of that same star, which impresses the souls it touches by the miracle of its appearance and leads them forward to worship God.

If on the other hand we earnestly ask ourselves whether the same threefold oblation is made by all who come to Christ in faith, shall we not discover a corresponding gift offering in the hearts of true believers? To acknowledge Christ's universal sovereignty is in fact to bring out gold from the treasury of one's soul; to believe God's only Son has made himself truly one with human nature is to offer myrrh, and to declare that he is in no way inferior to his Father in majesty is to worship him with frankincense.

*(Tractate 36, 1-2: CCL 138, 195-96)*

---

**Leo the Great** (c. 400-61) was elected pope in 440. At a time of general disorder he did much to strengthen the influence of the Roman see. Although he was not a profound theologian, Leo's teaching is clear and forceful. His Tome was accepted as a statement of Christological orthodoxy at the Council of Chalcedon (451). One hundred and forty-three of his letters and ninety-six sermons have survived. The latter, which cover the whole of the liturgical year, have been published in a critical edition.

# Baptism of the Lord

*Gospel:* Mark 1:7-11

You are my Son, the beloved; my favor rests on you.

*Commentary:* Ephrem

Today the Source of all the graces of baptism comes himself to be baptized in the river Jordan, there to make himself known to the world. Seeing him approach, John stretches out his hand to hold him back, protesting: Lord, by your own baptism you sanctify all others; yours is the true baptism, the source of perfect holiness. How can you wish to submit to mine?

But the Lord replies, I wish it to be so. Come and baptize me; do as I wish, for surely you cannot refuse me. Why do you hesitate, why are you so afraid? Do you not realize that the baptism I ask for is mine by every right? By my baptism the waters will be sanctified, receiving from me fire and the Holy Spirit. Unless I am immersed in them they will never be empowered to bring forth children to eternal life. There is every reason for you to let me have my way and do what I am asking you to do. Did I not baptize you when you were in your mother's womb? Now it is your turn to baptize me in the Jordan. So come, then, carry out your appointed task.

To this John answers, Your servant is utterly helpless. Savior of all, have mercy on me! I am not fit even to unfasten your sandal straps, let alone to lay my hand upon your venerable head. But I hear your command, Lord, and in obedience to your word I come to give you that baptism to which your own love impels you. Man of dust that I am, let deepest reverence enfold me when I behold the height to which I have been called—even to laying my hand on the head of my Maker!

See the hosts of heaven hushed and still, as the all-holy Bridegroom goes down into the Jordan. No sooner is he baptized than he comes up from the waters, his splendor shining forth over the earth. The gates of heaven are opened, and the Father's voice is heard: *This is my beloved Son in whom I am well pleased.* All who are present stand in awe as they watch the Spirit descend to bear witness to him. O come, all you peoples, worship him! Praise to you, Lord, for your glorious epiphany which brings joy to us all! The whole world has become radiant with the light of your manifestation.

*(Hymn 14, 6-8.14.32.36-37.47-50:*
*Edit. Lamy 1, 117-18.124.27)*

---

**Ephrem** (c. 306-73), the only Syrian Father who is honored as a doctor of the Church, was ordained deacon at Edessa in 363, and gave an outstanding example of a deacon's life and work. Most of his exegetical, dogmatic, controversial, and ascetical writings are in verse. They provide a rich mine of information regarding the faith and practice of the early Syrian Church. The poetry of Ephrem greatly influenced the development of Syriac and Greek hymnography.

# First Sunday of Lent

*Gospel:* Mark 1:12-15

He was tempted by Satan, and the angels looked after him.

*Commentary:* John Justus Landsberg

Everything the Lord Jesus decided to do, everything he chose to endure, was ordained by him for our instruction, our correction, and our advantage; and since he knew that the teaching and consolation we should derive from it all was far from negligible, he was loath to let slip any opportunity that might profit us. And so when he was led out into the wilderness there is no doubt that his guide was the Holy Spirit whose intention was to take him to a place where he would be exposed to temptation, a place where the devil would have the audacity to accost him and put him to the test. The circumstances were so greatly in the devil's favor that he was prompted to capitalize on them: here was Jesus alone, at prayer, physically worn out by fasting and abstinence. A chance indeed to find out whether this man really was the Christ, whether or not he was the Son of God.

From this episode therefore our first lesson is that human life on earth is a life of warfare, and the first thing Christians must expect is to be tempted by the devil. As Scripture tells us, we have to be prepared for temptation, for it is written: *When you enter God's service, prepare your soul for an ordeal.* For this reason, the Lord desires the newly baptized and recent converts to find comfort in his own example. Reading in the gospel that Christ too was tempted by the devil immediately after he was baptized, they will not grow fainthearted and fearful if they experience keener temptations from the devil after their conversion or baptism than before—even if persecution should be their lot.

The second lesson Christ desires to impress upon us by his own example is that we should not lightly expose ourselves to temptation, for we read that it was the Holy Spirit who led Jesus into the wilderness. Mindful of our frailty rather, we must be on the watch, praying not to be put to the test, and keeping ourselves clear of every occasion of temptation.

*(Complete Works I [1888] 120)*

---

**Landsberg, John Justus** (1489/90-1539), so called from the place of his birth in Bavaria, received the degree of Bachelor of Arts in Cologne, and then entered Saint Barbara's, the celebrated charterhouse there. He made his profession in 1509, and in due course was ordained a priest. From 1530 to 1534/35 he was prior of the charterhouse of Vogelsang, and at the same time preacher at the court of John III, duke of Juliers, Cleeves, and Berg, an unusual function for a Carthusian. Landsberg was one of the best spiritual writers of his day, the chief characteristic of his spirituality being the contemplation of Christ, the man-God, in his life, and in his passion and death. Landsberg was the editor of the works of Saint Gertrude, the great apostle in the middle ages of devotion to the Heart of Jesus, and he himself was one of the earliest promoters of this devotion.

# Second Sunday of Lent

*Gospel:* Mark 9:2-10

This is my Son, the beloved; listen to him.

*Commentary:* Ephrem

Jesus took the three apostles up to the mountain for three reasons: first, to show them the glory of his divinity, then to declare himself Israel's redeemer as he had already foretold by the prophets, and thirdly to prevent the apostles' being scandalized at seeing him soon afterward enduring those human sufferings which he had freely accepted for our sake. The apostles knew that Jesus was a man; they did not know that he was God. To their knowledge he was the son of Mary, a man who shared their daily life in this world. On the mountain he revealed to them that he was the Son of God, that he was in fact God himself. Peter, James, and John were familiar with the sight of their master eating and drinking, working and taking rest, growing tired and falling asleep, experiencing fear and breaking out in sweat. All these things were natural to his humanity, not to his divinity. He therefore took them up onto the mountain so that they could hear his Father's voice calling him Son, and he could show them that he was truly the Son of God and was himself divine.

He took them up onto the mountain in order to show them his kingship before they witnessed his passion, to let them see his mighty power before they watched his death, to reveal his glory to them before they beheld his humiliation. Then when the Jews took him captive and condemned him to the cross, the apostles would understand that it was not for any lack of power on his part that Jesus allowed himself to be crucified by his enemies, but because he had freely chosen to suffer in that way for the world's salvation. He took them up onto the mountain before his resurrection and showed them the glory of his divinity, so that when he rose from the dead in that same divine glory they would realize that this was not something given him as a reward for his labor, as if he were previously without it. That glory had been his with the Father from all eternity, as is clear from his words on approaching his freely chosen passion: *Father, glorify me now with the glory I had with you before the world was made.*

*(Sermon 16 on the Transfiguration, 1, 3, 4)*

---

**Ephrem** (c. 306-73), the only Syrian Father who is honored as a doctor of the Church, was ordained deacon at Edessa in 363, and gave an outstanding example of a deacon's life and work. Most of his exegetical, dogmatic, controversial, and ascetical writings are in verse. They provide a rich mine of information regarding the faith and practice of the early Syrian Church. The poetry of Ephrem greatly influenced the development of Syriac and Greek hymnography.

# Third Sunday of Lent

*Gospel:* John 2:13-25

Destroy this sanctuary and in three days I will raise it up.

*Commentary:* Augustine

God's temple is holy, and you are that temple: all you who believe in Christ and whose belief makes you love him. Real belief in Christ means love of Christ: it is not the belief of the demons who believed without loving and therefore despite their belief said: *What do you want with us, Son of God?* No; let our belief be full of love for him we believe in, so that instead of saying: *What do you want with us,* we may rather say: We belong to you, you have redeemed us. All who believe in this way are like the living stones which go to build God's temple, and like the rot-proof timber used in the framework of the ark which the flood waters could not submerge. It is in this temple, that is, in ourselves, that prayer is addressed to God and heard by him.

But to pray in God's temple we must pray in the peace of the Church, in the unity of the body of Christ, which is made up of many believers throughout the world. When we pray in this temple our prayers are heard, because whoever prays in the peace of the Church prays in spirit and in truth.

Our Lord's driving out of the temple people who were seeking their own ends, who came to the temple to buy and sell, is symbolic. For if that temple was a symbol it obviously follows that the body of Christ, the true temple of which the other was an image, has within it some who are buyers and sellers, or in other words, people who are seeking their own interests and not those of Jesus Christ.

But the temple was not destroyed by the people who wanted to turn the house of God into a den of thieves, and neither will those who live evil lives in the Catholic Church and do all they can to convert God's house into a robber's den succeed in destroying the temple. The time

34

will come when they will be driven out by a whip made of their own sins.

The temple of God, this body of Christ, this assembly of believers, has but one voice, and sings the psalms as though it were but one person. If we wish, it is our voice; if we wish, we may listen to the singer with our ears and ourselves sing in our hearts. But if we choose not to do so it will mean that we are like buyers and sellers, preoccupied with our own interests.

*(Expositions of the Psalms 130, 1-2: CCL 40, 1898-1900)*

---

**Augustine** (354-430) was born at Thagaste in Africa and received a Christian education, although he was not baptized until 387. In 391 he was ordained priest and in 395 he became coadjutor bishop to Valerius of Hippo, whom he succeeded in 396. Augustine's theology was formulated in the course of his struggle with three heresies: Manichaeism, Donatism, and Pelagianism. His writings are voluminous and his influence on subsequent theology immense. He molded the thought of the Middle Ages down to the thirteenth century. Yet he was above all a pastor and a great spiritual writer.

# Fourth Sunday of Lent

*Gospel:* John 3:14-21

God loved the world so much that he gave his only Son.

*Commentary:* John Chrysostom

Although we praise our common Lord for all kinds of reasons, we praise and glorify him above all for the cross. It fills us with awe to see him dying like one accursed. It is this death for people like ourselves that Paul constantly regards as the sign of Christ's love for us. He passes over everything else that Christ did for our advantage and consolation and dwells incessantly on the cross. *The proof of God's love for us,* he says, *is that Christ died for us while we were still sinners.* Then in the following sentence he gives us the highest ground for hope: *If, when we were alienated from God, we were reconciled to him by the death of his Son, how much more, now that we are reconciled, shall we be saved by his life!* It is this above all that made Paul so proud, so happy, so full of joy and exultation, when he wrote to the Galatians: *God forbid that I should glory in anything but the cross of our Lord Jesus Christ.* What wonder, indeed, if Paul rejoices and glories in the cross, when the Lord himself spoke of his passion as his glory. *Father,* he prayed, the hour has come: glorify your Son.

The disciple who wrote those words also told us that the Holy Spirit had not yet come to them because Jesus was not yet glorified, calling the cross glory. And when he wanted to show God's love did he do so by referring to signs, wonders, or miracles of any sort? By no means: he pointed to the cross, saying: *God so loved the world that he gave his only Son, that all who believe in him might not perish but have eternal life.* And Paul writes: *Since he did not spare his own Son, but gave him up for us all, how can he fail to lavish every other gift upon us?* And in his exhortation to humility he uses the same example, saying: *"You should have the same dispositions as you find in Christ*

36

*Jesus. Although his nature was divine, he did not cling to his equality with God, but emptied himself to assume the condition of a slave. Bearing the human likeness, sharing the human lot, he humbled himself and was obedient even to the point of dying—dying on a cross!*

Returning to the subject of love, Paul again urges his hearers to *love one another, even as Christ loved us, and gave himself up for us as a fragrant offering and sacrifice to God.* And Christ himself showed how the cross was his chief preoccupation, and how much he longed to suffer. In his ignorance, Peter, first of the Twelve, foundation of the Church, leader of the Apostles, protested: *God forbid, Lord! This shall never happen to you!* Listen to what Christ called him: *Get behind me, Satan. You are an obstacle in my way,* proving by the strength of his reprimand his great eagerness to suffer on the cross.

*(Treatise on Providence 17, 1-8: SC 79, 225-29)*

---

**John Chrysostom** (c. 347-407) was born at Antioch and studied under Diodore of Tarsus, the leader of the Antiochene school of theology. After a period of great austerity as a hermit, he returned to Antioch where he was ordained deacon in 381 and priest in 386. From 386 to 397 it was his duty to preach in the principal church of the city, and his best homilies, which earned the title "Chrysostomos" or "the golden-mouthed," were preached at this time. In 397 Chrysostom became patriarch of Constantinople, where his efforts to reform the court, clergy, and people led to his exile in 404 and finally to his death from the hardships imposed on him. Chrysostom stressed the divinity of Christ against the Arians and his full humanity against the Apollinarians, but he had no speculative bent. He was above all a pastor of souls, and was one of the most attractive personalities of the early Church.

# Fifth Sunday of Lent

*Gospel:* John 12:20-33

If a grain of wheat falls on the ground and dies, it yields a rich harvest.

*Commentary:* Cyril of Alexandria

As the firstfruits of our renewed humanity, Christ escaped the curse of the law precisely by becoming accursed for our sake. He overcame the forces of corruption by himself becoming once more *free among the dead.* He trampled death under foot and came to life again, and then he ascended to the Father as an offering, the firstfruits, as it were, of the human race. *He ascended,* as Scripture says, *not to a sanctuary made by human hands, a mere copy of the real one, but into heaven itself, to appear in God's presence on our behalf.* He is the life-giving bread that came down from heaven, and by offering himself to God the Father as a fragrant sacrifice for our sake, he also delivers us from our sins and frees us from the faults that we commit through ignorance. We can understand this best if we think of him as symbolized by the calf that used to be slain as a holocaust and by the goat that was sacrificed for our sins committed through ignorance. For our sake, to blot out the sins of the world, he laid down his life.

Recognized then in bread as life and the giver of life, in the calf as a holocaust offered by himself to God the Father as an appeasing fragrance, in the goat as one who became sin for our sake and was slain for our transgressions, Christ is also symbolized in another way by a sheaf of grain, as a brief explanation will show.

The human race may be compared to spikes of wheat in a field, rising, as it were, from the earth, awaiting their full growth and development, and then in time being cut down by the reaper, which is death. The comparison is apt, since Christ himself spoke of our race in this way when he said to his holy disciples: *Do you not say, "Four months and it will be harvest time?" Look at the fields I tell you, they are already white and ready for harvesting. The reaper is already receiving his wages and bringing in a crop for eternal life.*

Now Christ became like one of us; he sprang from the holy Virgin like a spike of wheat from the ground. Indeed, he spoke of himself as a grain of wheat when he said: *I tell you truly, unless a grain of wheat falls into the ground and dies, it remains as it was, a single grain; but if it dies its yield is very great.* And so, like a sheaf of grain, the firstfruits, as it were, of the earth, he offered himself to the Father for our sake.

For we do not think of a spike of wheat, any more than we do of ourselves, in isolation. We think of it rather as part of a sheaf, which is a single bundle made up of many spikes. The spikes have to be gathered into a bundle before they can be used, and this is the key to the mystery they represent, the mystery of Christ who, though one, appears in the image of a sheaf to be made up of many, as in fact he is. Spiritually, he contains in himself all believers. *As we have been raised up with him,* writes Saint Paul, *so we have also been enthroned with him in heaven.* He is a human being like ourselves, and this has made us one body with him, the body being the bond that unites us. We can say, therefore, that in him we are all one, and indeed he himself says to God, his heavenly Father: *It is my desire that as I and you are one, so they also may be one in us.*

*(Commentary on Numbers 2: PG 69, 617-24)*

---

**Cyril of Alexandria** (d. 444) succeeded his uncle Theophilus as patriarch in 412. Until 428 the pen of this brilliant theologian was employed in exegesis and polemics against the Arians; after that date it was devoted almost entirely to refuting the Nestorian heresy. The teaching of Nestorius was condemned in 431 by the Council of Ephesus at which Cyril presided, and Mary's title, Mother of God, was solemnly recognized. The incarnation is central to Cyril's theology. Only if Christ is consubstantial with the Father and with us can he save us, for the meeting ground between God and ourselves is the flesh of Christ. Through our kinship with Christ, the Word made flesh, we become children of God, and share in the filial relation of the Son with the Father.

# Passion Sunday

*Gospel:* Mark 11:1-10

Blessed is he who comes in the name of the Lord.

*Commentary:* Guerric of Igny

When Jesus entered Jerusalem like a triumphant conqueror, many were astonished at the majesty of his bearing; but when a short while afterward he entered upon his passion, his appearance was ignoble, an object of derision. If today's procession and passion are considered together, in the one Jesus appears as sublime and glorious, in the other as lowly and suffering. The procession makes us think of the honor reserved for a king, whereas the passion shows us the punishment due to a thief.

In the one Jesus is surrounded by glory and honor, in the other *he has neither dignity nor beauty.* In the one he is the joy of all and the glory of the people, in the other *the butt of men and the laughing stock of the people.* In the one he receives the acclamation: *Hosanna to the Son of David! Blessed is he who comes as the king of Israel;* in the other there are shouts that he is guilty of death and he is reviled for having set himself up as king of Israel.

In the procession the people meet Jesus with palm branches, in the passion they slap him in the face and strike his head with a rod. In the one they extol him with praises, in the other they heap insults upon him. In the one they compete to lay their clothes in his path, in the other he is stripped of his own clothes. In the one he is welcomed to Jerusalem as a just king and savior, in the other he is thrown out of the city as a criminal, condemned as an impostor. In the one he is mounted on an ass and accorded every mark of honor; in the other he hangs on the wood of the cross, torn by whips, pierced with wounds, and abandoned by his own. If, then, we want to follow our leader without stumbling through prosperity and through adversity, let us keep our eyes upon him, honored in the procession, undergoing ignominy and suffering in the passion, yet unshakably steadfast in all such changes of fortune.

Lord Jesus, you are the joy and salvation of the whole world; whether we see you seated on an ass or hanging on the cross, let each one of us bless and praise you, so that when we see you reigning on high we may praise you for ever and ever, for to you belong praise and honor throughout all ages. Amen.

*(Sermon 3 on Palm Sunday 2. 5: SC 202, 190-93.198-201)*

---

**Guerric of Igny** (c. 1070/80-1157), about whose early life little is known, probably received his education at the cathedral school of Tournai, perhaps under the influence of Odo of Cambrai (1087-92). He seems to have lived a retired life of prayer and study near the cathedral of Tournai. He paid a visit to Clairvaux to consult Saint Bernard, and is mentioned by him as a novice in a letter to Ogerius in 1125/1256. He became abbot of the Cistercian abbey of Igny, in the diocese of Rheims in 1138. A collection of fifty-four authentic sermons preached on Sundays and feast days have been edited. Guerric's spirituality was influenced by Origen.

# Easter Triduum

# *Evening Mass of the Lord's Supper*

*Gospel:* John 13:1-15

Now he showed how perfect was his love.

*Commentary:* Alonso de Orozco

How faithful a friend is Christ Jesus, a friend never unmindful of his own! Because *he loved them to the end* he gave them, as he was about to die, the uttermost proof of his love. Falling down before them he washed their feet, in order to leave both to them and to all his followers a supreme example of humility; and accordingly he told them, *I have given you this example so that you yourselves may deal with others as I have with you.* After that, we have no grounds for pride, creatures of earth and ashes as we are, since the God of eternal majesty has so abased and emptied himself as to perform a slave's office.

He went further, and gave a yet greater sign of his love by instituting this wonderful sacrament as a memorial of his sacred death. *Take this,* he said: *This is my body, which will be delivered up for you. Do this in memory of me.* These are burning words indeed; what ardent charity breathes through them! *Do this in memory of me.* Let it be to you a memorial of my whole life of shining purity, and a mirror of my laborious passion. Yes, I tell you, I have engraved you on my hands; more than that, the lance has carved you upon my heart, and I long to carry you in my inmost being as in a mother's womb. Respond to me, then, by celebrating this memorial of me and receiving my sacred body.

Let us make haste, dearly beloved, to wash our feet as speedily as we may, and with tears expunge the stains from our hearts by repentance, so that we may worthily approach the table of the King of Kings, Christ Jesus. As we eat the living bread which *has come down from heaven,* may he find us fit to draw from this divine food the richest of benefits. Christ Jesus himself has promised that *whoever eats this bread will live for ever*; may he then bestow this life upon us by his most gracious mercy, who lives and reigns with the Father and the Holy Spirit for all eternity. Amen.

*(Sermon 22 on Holy Thursday: Opera I, 456-57)*

---

**Alonso de Orozco** (1500-91) studied at the University of Salamanca before entering the Augustinian novitiate there. His main apostolates in the Order were preaching and writing, and although he was chosen as royal preacher at the Spanish court, he preferred to speak to poor and simple people. His religious life was marked by a spirit of fraternity, gospel simplicity and moderation in speech. As an ascetic and great mystic, he suffered crises and spiritual aridity from 1522-51. He was beatified by Pope Leo XIII in 1882.

# Good Friday

*Gospel:* John 18:1-19.42

The account of the passion of our Lord Jesus Christ.

*Commentary:* Leo the Great

When our Lord was handed over to the will of his cruel foes, they ordered him, in mockery of his royal dignity, to carry the instrument of his own torture. This was done to fulfil the prophecy of Isaiah: *A child is born for us, a son is given to us; sovereignty is laid upon his shoulders.* To the wicked, the sight of the Lord carrying his own cross was indeed an object of derision; but to the faithful a great mystery was revealed, for the cross was destined to become the scepter of his power. Here was the majestic spectacle of a glorious conqueror mightily overthrowing the hostile forces of the devil and nobly bearing the trophy of his victory. On the shoulders of his invincible patience he carried the sign of salvation for all the kingdoms of the earth to worship, as if on that day he would strengthen all his future disciples by the symbol of his work, and say to them: *Anyone who does not take up his cross and follow me is not worthy of me.*

It was not in the temple, whose cult was now at an end, that Christ, as the new and authentic sacrifice of reconciliation, offered himself to the Father; nor was it within the walls of the city doomed to destruction for its crimes. It was beyond the city gates, outside the camp, that he was crucified, in order that when the ancient sacrificial dispensation came to an end a new victim might be laid on a new altar, and the cross of Christ become the altar not of the temple, but of the world.

O the marvelous power of the cross, the glory of the passion! No tongue can fully describe it. Here we see the judgment seat of the Lord, here sentence is passed upon the world, and here the sovereignty of the Crucified is revealed. You drew all things to yourself, Lord, when you stretched out your hands all the day long to a people that denied and opposed you, until at last the whole world was brought to proclaim your majesty. You drew all things to yourself, Lord, when all the elements combined to pronounce judgment in execration of that crime; when the lights of heaven were darkened and the day was turned into night; when the land was shaken by unwonted earthquakes, and all creation refused to serve those wicked people. Yes, Lord, you drew all things to yourself. The veil of the temple was torn in two and the Holy of Holies taken away from those unworthy high priests. Figures gave way to reality, prophecy to manifestation, law to gospel. You drew all things to yourself in order that the worship of the whole human race could be celebrated everywhere in a sacramental form which would openly fulfil what had been enacted by means of veiled symbols in that single Jewish temple. Now that the multiplicity of animal sacrifices has ceased, the single offering of your body and blood takes the place of that diversity of victims, since you are the true Lamb of God who takes away the sins of the world, and in yourself you fulfil all the rites of the old law, so that as there is now a single sacrifice in place of all those victims, so there is a single kingdom formed of all the peoples of the earth.

*(Sermon 8 on the Passion of the Lord, 4-6: PL 54, 339-41)*

---

**Leo the Great** (c. 400-61) was elected pope in 440. At a time of general disorder he did much to strengthen the influence of the Roman see. Although he was not a profound theologian, Leo's teaching is clear and forceful. His Tome was accepted as a statement of Christological orthodoxy at the Council of Chalcedon (451). One hundred and forty-three of his letters and ninety-six sermons have survived. The latter, which cover the whole of the liturgical year, have been published in a critical edition.

# Easter Vigil

*Gospel:* Mark 16:1-8

Jesus of Nazareth, who was crucified, has risen.

*Commentary:* Basil of Seleucia

Christ descended into hell to liberate its captives. In one instant he destroyed all record of our ancient debt incurred under the law, in order to lead us to heaven where there is no death but only eternal life and righteousness.

By the baptism which you, the newly-enlightened, have just received, you now share in these blessings. Your initiation into the life of grace is the pledge of your resurrection. Your baptism is the promise of the life of heaven. By your immersion you imitated the burial of the Lord, but when you came out of the water you were conscious only of the reality of the resurrection.

Believe in this reality, of which previously you saw but the outward signs. Accept the assurance of Paul when he says: *If we have been united to Christ in a death like his, we shall be united to him also in a resurrection like his.* Baptism is the planting of the seed of immortality, a planting which takes place in the font and bears fruit in heaven. The grace of the Spirit works in a mysterious way in the font, and the outward appearance must not obscure the wonder of it. Although water serves as the instrument, it is grace which gives rebirth. Grace transforms all who are placed in the font as the seed is transformed in the womb. It refashions all who go down into the water as metal is recast in a furnace. It reveals to them the mysteries of immortality; it seals them with the pledge of resurrection.

These wonderful mysteries are symbolized for you, the newly-enlightened, even in the garments you wear. See how you are clothed in the outward signs of these blessings. The radiant brightness of your robe stands for incorruptibility. The white band encircling your head like a diadem proclaims your liberty. In your hand you hold the sign of your victory over the devil. Christ is showing you that you have risen from the dead. He does this now in a symbolic way, but soon he will reveal the full reality if we keep the garment of faith undefiled and do not let sin extinguish the lamp of grace. If we preserve the crown of the Spirit the Lord will call from heaven in a voice of tremendous majesty, yet full of tenderness: *Come, blessed of my Father, take possession of the kingdom prepared for you since the beginning of the world.* To him be glory and power for ever, through endless ages, amen.

*(Easter Homily: PG 28, 1079-82)*

---

**Basil of Seleucia** (d. 459) became archbishop of Seleucia about the year 440. He is remembered for his fluctuating attitude in the events which preceded the Council of Chalcedon in 451. He voted against Monophysitism at the Synod of Constantinople in 448, but at the "Robber Synod" of Ephesus in 449 gave his support to Eutyches, the originator of Monophysitism. Then at the Council of Chalcedon he signed the Tome of Saint Leo, which condemned Eutyches. Thirty-nine of Basil's homilies have been preserved. They show his concern to place the exegesis of his time within the reach of all.

# Easter Sunday

*Gospel:* John 20:1-9

The teaching of Scripture is that he must rise from the dead.

*Commentary:* Attributed to Epiphanius

T*his is the day that the Lord has made: let us rejoice and be glad in it* with a spiritual gladness pleasing to God. This is our greatest feast, one that is celebrated by all the world, a feast of renewal and salvation.

Today God has fulfilled all types, symbols, and prophecies. *Christ our Passover,* the true Passover, *is sacrificed,* and in Christ all is made new: there is a new creation, a new faith, new laws, a new people of God, a new Israel in place of the old, a new Passover, a new and spiritual circumcision, a new and unbloody sacrifice, a new divine covenant.

We too must be renewed today; we must renew a right spirit within our hearts and so prepare to enter into the mysteries of this new and perfect feast and to exult in this day's heavenly joy. We shall then depart as initiates of the mysteries of the new Passover, mysteries fulfilling those of the old dispensation and which will never be superseded. We shall see how great the difference is between the Jewish mysteries and ours and be able to compare the type with the reality. With these thoughts, let us begin our meditation upon Christ, our Passover, and upon his mission.

Of old, Moses, the lawgiver, was sent by God from a high mountain to save his people and to symbolize the law. The Lord, the lawgiver, was also sent, God by God, mountain from the highest mountain of heaven, to save our people and to *be* the law. Moses delivered his people from Pharaoh and the Egyptians, but Christ has delivered us from the devil and evil spirits. Moses made peace between his two contending brethren, but Christ has made peace between his two peoples and united heaven and earth.

Israel kept the symbolic Passover by night: we celebrate the true Passover by the light of day. They kept it in the evening of the day: we keep it in the evening of the world. Then the doorposts and lintels were sprinkled with blood: now it is the hearts of the faithful that are sealed with the blood of Christ. Then the sacrifice was offered by night and the crossing of the Red Sea took place at night, but now we are saved by the Red Sea of baptism that glows with the fire of the Spirit. In baptism the Spirit of God truly descends and appears on the waters in which the head of the serpent, the prince of serpents and demons, is crushed. Moses gave Israel its baptism by night and a cloud overshadowed the people, but it is the power of the Most High that overshadows the people of Christ.

Moses had recourse to a rock of this creation, but we turn to the rock of faith. Then, the tablets of the law were broken in pieces as a sign that the law would be abrogated: now, the laws of God stand for ever. Then, the making of a molten calf brought retribution on the people: now, the sacrifice of the Lamb of God is the salvation of the people. Then, water poured from the rock when it was struck by a rod: now, from the pierced and lifegiving side of the rock which is Christ, both blood and water flow. The Jews of old were given quails from heaven: our gift from on high is the Dove, the Holy Spirit. They fed on perishable manna and died: the bread that we eat brings us everlasting life.

*(Homily 3 on Christ's Resurrection: PG 43, 466-70)*

# Second Sunday of Easter

*Gospel:* John 20:19-31

After eight days Jesus came in and stood among them.

*Commentary:* Cyril of Alexandria

Thomas' profession of faith came swiftly when, eight days after he had declared his unwillingness to believe, Christ showed him his side and the nail marks in his hands and removed every possible doubt.

Our Lord Jesus Christ had miraculously entered the room when the doors were closed. As this would have been impossible for an ordinary earthly body he reassured Thomas, and through him the other disciples, by letting him see his side and the wounds in his flesh.

Only Thomas is reported to have said: *Unless my hands touch the marks of the nails and I see them, and unless I put my hand into his side, I will not believe;* yet to some extent all the disciples were guilty of disbelief. Doubt remained in their minds even after they had told Thomas that they had seen the Lord. Saint Luke's account says that *while they stood amazed, torn between joy and disbelief, Christ said to them: "Have you anything to eat?" They gave him a piece of broiled fish and part of a honeycomb, which he took and ate before their eyes.* This surely proves that it was not only in the mind of blessed Thomas that disbelieving thoughts still lurked, but in the minds of the other disciples as well. It was their very astonishment that made them slow to believe, but when it became impossible to disbelieve what they could see with their own eyes, blessed Thomas made his profession of faith: *My Lord and my God.*

Jesus said to him: "Because you have seen me, Thomas, you have believed. Blessed are those who have not seen, and yet believe." There was a wonderful providence behind these words of the Savior, and they can be of very great help to us. They show once again how much he cares for our souls, for he is good and as Scripture says: He wants

50

everyone to be saved and to come to knowledge of the truth. Even so, this saying of his may surprise us.

As always, Christ had to be patient with Thomas when he said he would not believe and with the other disciples too when they thought they were seeing a ghost. Because of his desire to convince the whole world, he most willingly showed them the marks of the nails and the wound in his side; because he wished those who needed such signs as a support for their faith to have no possible reason for doubt, he even took food although he had no need for it.

But when anyone accepts what he has not seen, believing on the word of his teacher, the faith by which he honors the one his teacher proclaims to him is worthy of great praise. Blessed, therefore, is everyone who believes the message of the holy apostles who, as Luke says, were eyewitnesses of Christ's actions and ministers of the word. If we desire eternal life and long for a dwelling place in heaven, we must listen to them.

*(Commentary on John's Gospel 12, 22: PG 74, 729-36)*

---

**Cyril of Alexandria** (d. 444) succeeded his uncle Theophilus as patriarch in 412. Until 428 the pen of this brilliant theologian was employed in exegesis and polemics against the Arians; after that date it was devoted almost entirely to refuting the Nestorian heresy. The teaching of Nestorius was condemned in 431 by the Council of Ephesus at which Cyril presided, and Mary's title, Mother of God, was solemnly recognized. The incarnation is central to Cyril's theology. Only if Christ is consubstantial with the Father and with us can he save us, for the meeting ground between God and ourselves is the flesh of Christ. Through our kinship with Christ, the Word made flesh, we become children of God, and share in the filial relation of the Son with the Father.

# Third Sunday of Easter

*Gospel:* Luke 24:35-48

It was written that the Christ would suffer and on the third day rise from the dead.

*Commentary:* Augustine

Christ rose from the tomb with his wounds healed, though their scars remained. He knew it would be good for his disciples if he retained the scars, for those scars would heal the wound in their hearts. What wound do I mean? The wound of disbelief; for even when he appeared before their eyes and showed them his true body, they still took him for a disembodied spirit. So he showed himself to his disciples. When we say "himself," what precisely do we mean? We mean Christ as head of his Church. He foresaw the Church extending throughout the world, a vision his disciples could not yet share. However, in showing them the head, he was promising them the body too. What, in fact, were his next words to them? All these things I told you while I was still among you, meaning: I still had to face death when I was among you as a mortal among mortals. But now I no longer live among you as before; never again shall I have to die as mortals do. What I was telling you, then, was that everything that had been written about me had to be fulfilled.

Then he opened their minds to understand the meaning of it all, explaining to them that *it had been decreed that Christ should suffer and on the third day rise from the dead.* But all this they had themselves seen: with their own eyes they had seen him suffer, seen him hanging on the cross, and now, after his resurrection, they could see him standing before them alive. What, then can it have been that they were still incapable of seeing? It was his body, the Church. Him they could see well enough, but the Church not at all. The bridegroom they could see, but the bride was still hidden from them. Nevertheless, he promised her to them. *Thus it is written: Christ must suffer and on the third day rise from the dead.* So much for the bridegroom, but what of the bride? *In his name repentance must be preached to every nation on earth for the forgiveness of sins, beginning at Jerusalem.* This is what the disciples had not yet seen: they had no vision yet of the Church spreading from Jerusalem over the whole world. But they could see the head before them, and when he spoke to them of the body, they believed him.

Now we too find ourselves in a situation not unlike theirs: we can see something which was not visible to them, while they could see something not visible to us. We can see the Church extending throughout the world today, something that was withheld from them, but Christ, who in his human body was perceptible to them, cannot be seen by us. And just as they, seeing his human flesh, were enabled to believe in his mystical body, so now we, seeing his mystical body, should be able to believe in the head. Just as the sight of the risen Christ helped the disciples to believe in the Church that was to follow, so the spectacle of that same Church helps to confirm our faith in the resurrection of Christ. The faith of the disciples was made complete, and so is ours: theirs by the sight of the head, ours by the sight of the body. But to them and to us alike the whole Christ is revealed, though neither to them nor to us has it yet been granted to see him in his entirety. For while they could see the head alone with their physical eyes and the body only with the eyes of faith, we can see only the body and have to take the head on trust. Nevertheless, Christ is absent from no one; he is wholly present in all of us, even though he still waits for his body to be completed.

*(Sermon 116, 1.5-6: PL 38, 657-60)*

---

**Augustine** (354-430) was born at Thagaste in Africa and received a Christian education, although he was not baptized until 387. In 391 he was ordained priest and in 395 he became coadjutor bishop to Valerius of Hippo, whom he succeeded in 396. Augustine's theology was formulated in the course of his struggle with three heresies: Manichaeism, Donatism, and Pelagianism. His writings are voluminous and his influence on subsequent theology immense. He molded the thought of the Middle Ages down to the thirteenth century. Yet he was above all a pastor and a great spiritual writer.

# Fourth Sunday of Easter

*Gospel:* John 10:11-18

The Good Shepherd lays down his life for his sheep.

*Commentary:* Basil of Seleucia

*I am the Good Shepherd. The Good Shepherd lays down his life for his sheep.* For the sake of his flock the shepherd was sacrificed as though he were a sheep. He did not refuse death; he did not destroy his executioners as he had the power to do, for his passion was not forced upon him. He laid down his life for his sheep of his own free will. *I have the power to lay it down,* he said, *and I have the power to take it up again.* By his passion he made atonement for our evil passions, by his death he cured our death, by his tomb he robbed the tomb, by the nails that pierced his flesh he destroyed the foundations of hell.

Death held sway until Christ died. The grave was bitter, our prison was indestructible, until the shepherd went down and brought to his sheep confined there the good news of their release. His appearance among them gave them a pledge of their resurrection and called them to a new life beyond the grave. *The Good Shepherd lays down his life for his sheep and so seeks to win their love.*

Now to love Christ means to obey his commands. The shepherd knows how to separate goats from sheep. The gospel says that *all nations will be assembled before him and he will separate people from one another, as the Good Shepherd separates the sheep from the goats. He will place the sheep on his right hand, and the goats on his left, and he will say to those on his right hand, "Come, blessed of my Father, inherit the kingdom prepared for you from the foundation of the world."* What had they done to earn this invitation? *I was hungry and you gave me food; I was thirsty and you gave me drink. I was a stranger and you welcomed me, naked and you clothed me.* What you give to those who are mine, you will receive back from me. Because they are naked, strangers, homeless, and poor, so am I, and in supplying their needs you show kindness to me. It is I who am afflicted when they cry out. Win the judge over by gifts before you come to trial. Provide him with grounds for showing clemency, give him some reason to acquit you. Otherwise you will be among those on his left hand who hear the terrible sentence: *Depart from me with your curse upon you to the eternal fire prepared for the devil and his angels.*

What are the sins for which we would be condemned with the devil? I was hungry and you gave me no food; I was thirsty and you gave me no drink; I was a stranger and you did not welcome me; naked and you did not clothe me. Who could turn away from his own shepherd when he was hungry, or fail to notice when his future judge lacked necessary clothing? Who could condemn the judge of the whole world to suffer thirst? Christ will accept even the gift of the poor and for a small gift grant remission of long punishment. Let us put out the fire with mercy and avert the sentence that hangs over us by showing love for one another. Let us be compassionate toward one another and forgiving, as God has forgiven us in Christ. To him be glory and power for ever. Amen.

*(Homily 26, 2: PG 85, 306-07)*

---

**Basil of Seleucia** (c. 459) became archbishop of Seleucia about the year 440. He is remembered for his fluctuating attitude in the events which preceded the Council of Chalcedon in 451. He voted against Monophysitism at the Synod of Constantinople in 448, but at the "Robber Synod" of Ephesus in 449 gave his support to Eutyches, the originator of Monophysitism. Then at the Council of Chalcedon he signed the Tome of Saint Leo, which condemned Eutyches. Thirty-nine of Basil's homilies have been preserved. They show his concern to place the exegesis of his time within the reach of all.

# Fifth Sunday of Easter

*Gospel:* John 15:1-8

Whoever lives in me, as I live in him, bears much fruit.

*Commentary:* Augustine

The passage from the gospel in which the Lord calls himself the vine and his disciples the branches affirms in its own way that, as mediator between God and the human race, the man Christ Jesus is head of the Church and we are his members. It is beyond dispute that a vine and its branches are of one and the same stock. Since Christ, therefore, possessed a divine nature not shared by ourselves, he became man precisely in order that in his own person there might be a vine of human stock whose branches we could become.

*Dwell in me,* said Jesus, *and I will dwell in you.* His disciples, however, do not dwell in Christ in the same way as Christ dwells in them. In either case, the benefit is theirs, not his. If branches are attached to a vine, it is not to confer any advantage on the vine; it is rather that the branches themselves may draw their sustenance from the vine. The vine is attached to the branches to provide them with their vital nourishment, not to receive anything from them. In the same way Christ's presence in his disciples and their presence in him both profit the disciples rather than Christ. If a branch is cut off, another can grow from the life-giving root; but once severed from the root no branch can remain alive.

The incarnate Truth goes on to say: *I am the vine, you are the branches. Whoever dwells in me and I in him yields fruit in plenty, because without me you can do nothing.* These are words to be weighed and pondered continually. Someone hearing Jesus say, *he yields fruit in plenty,* might perhaps think that a branch can bear at least a certain amount of fruit on its own. Our Lord's words, however, were not: *You can do little without me,* but: *You can do nothing.* Little fruit or plenty, there can be neither without him, because without him nothing can be done. Even if a branch does produce a little fruit, the

56

vinedresser prunes it away so that it may produce more. But if the branch does not remain attached to the vine and draw its life from the root, it can bear no fruit at all.

Now, although Christ could not be the vine if he were not human, he could not offer such a grace to his branches if he were not at the same time divine. Since without this grace it is impossible to have life and consequently death is the result of one's free choice, he said: *Whoever does not dwell in me will be thrown away like a branch and will wither, to be gathered in and cast on the fire to burn.* And so the shame incurred by those branches that refuse to dwell in the vine is in direct proportion to the glory they will have if they do remain in him.

*If you dwell in me,* said Jesus, *and my words dwell in you, you will ask for whatever you desire and it will be yours.* Can a person dwelling in Christ desire anything out of harmony with Christ? The very fact that people dwell in their Savior must mean that they have no desire that is opposed to their salvation. And yet we do indeed desire one thing insofar as we are in Christ, and another insofar as we are still in this world. Because of our sojourn here below, a thought sometimes steals into our ignorant minds to ask for something which cannot be good for us. But this may not be, if we are dwelling in Christ. He does what we ask only if it is for our good. To dwell in him, therefore, is to have his words dwelling in us; whatever we desire we shall then ask for, and it will be given us.

*(Homily on the Gospel of John 80, 1; 81, 1.3.4:*
*CCL 36, 527.530-31)*

---

**Augustine** (354-430) was born at Thagaste in Africa and received a Christian education, although he was not baptized until 387. In 391 he was ordained priest and in 395 he became coadjutor bishop to Valerius of Hippo, whom he succeeded in 396. Augustine's theology was formulated in the course of his struggle with three heresies: Manichaeism, Donatism, and Pelagianism. His writings are voluminous and his influence on subsequent theology immense. He molded the thought of the Middle Ages down to the thirteenth century. Yet he was above all a pastor and a great spiritual writer.

# Sixth Sunday of Easter

*Gospel:* John 15:9-17

No one has greater love than this, to lay down one's life for one's friends.

*Commentary:* Thomas More

L et us deeply consider the love of our Savior Christ who so loved his own unto the end that for their sakes he willingly suffered that painful end, and therein declared the highest degree of love that can be. For, as he himself says: *A greater love no one has than to give his life for his friends.* This is indeed the greatest love that ever anyone had. But yet had our Savior a greater, for he gave his for both friend and foe.

But what a difference is there now, between this faithful love of his and other kinds of false and fickle love found in this wretched world. The flatterer pretends to love you because he dines well with you. But now if adversity so diminish your possessions that he find your table not laid, then—farewell, adieu—your brother flatterer is gone and gets himself to some other table. And he might even sometime turn into your enemy and cruelly speak evil of you.

Who can in adversity be sure of many of his friends when our Savior himself was, at his capture, left alone and forsaken by his? When you go forth who will go with you? If you were a king would not all your realm send you on your way alone and then forget you? Will not your own family let you depart a naked, feeble soul, you know not whither?

Let us all in time, then, learn to love as we should, God above all things, and all other things for him. And whatsoever love be not referred to that end, namely, to the good pleasure of God, is a very vain and unfruitful love. And whatsoever love we bear to any creature whereby we love God the less, that love is a loathesome love and hinders us from heaven. Love no child of yours so tenderly but that you could be content to sacrifice it to God, as Abraham was ready with

58

Isaac, if God so commanded you. And since God will not do so, offer your child in another way to God's service. For whatever we love that makes us break God's commandment, we love better than God, and that is a love deadly and damnable. Now, since our Lord has so loved us, for our salvation, let us diligently call for his grace that in return for his great love we be not found ungrateful.

*("A Treatise upon the Passion, Christ's Love Unto the End," Homily 1. Partially modernized)*

---

**More, Thomas** (1477/78-1535) was born in London. After spending four years in the London Charterhouse without taking vows, he followed his father into the legal profession, eventually becoming Lord Chancellor of England. His wit and learning made his house in Chelsea the meeting place for scholars such as Erasmus, Colet, and Grocyn. By the integrity of his public life, his virtues as husband and father, and his piety, More gave a shining example of what a Christian layman should be. His writings include many letters, refutations of the heresies of the time, and devotional works, but the book that made him famous all over Europe was his *Utopia*. More refused to sign an oath accepting the Act of Succession because it would have involved the repudiation of papal supremacy. For this he was imprisoned in the Tower of London for fifteen months and finally died a martyr's death.

# Ascension

*Gospel:* Mark 16:15-20

The Lord Jesus was taken up into heaven and is seated at the right hand of God.

## *Commentary:* Leo the Great

The sacred work of our salvation was of such value in the sight of the Creator of the universe that he counted it worth the shedding of his own blood. From the day of his birth until his passion and death this work was carried out in conditions of self-abasement; and although he showed many signs of his divinity even when he bore the form of a slave, yet, strictly speaking, the events of that time were concerned with proving the reality of the humanity he had assumed. But he was innocent of any sin, and so when death launched its attack upon him he burst its bonds and robbed it of its power. After his passion weakness was turned into strength, mortality into eternal life, and disgrace into glory. Of all this our Lord Jesus Christ gave ample proof in the sight of many, until at last he entered heaven in triumph, bearing with him the trophy of his victory over death.

And so while at Easter it was the Lord's resurrection which was the cause of our joy, our present rejoicing is on account of his ascension into heaven. With all due solemnity we are commemorating that day on which our poor human nature was carried up in Christ above all the hosts of heaven, above all the ranks of angels, beyond the highest heavenly powers to the very throne of God the Father. It is upon this ordered structure of divine acts that we have been firmly established, so that the grace of God may show itself still more marvelous when, in spite of the withdrawal from our sight of everything that is rightly felt to command our reverence, faith does not fail, hope is not shaken, charity does not grow cold.

For such is the power of great minds, such the light of truly believing souls, that they put unhesitating faith in what is not seen with the bodily eye; they fix their desires on what is beyond sight. Such fidelity could never be born in our hearts, nor could anyone be justified by faith, if our salvation lay only in what was visible. This is why Christ said to the man who seemed doubtful about his resurrection unless he could see and touch the marks of his passion in his very flesh: *You believe because you see me; blessed are those who have not seen and yet believe.*

It was in order that we might be capable of such blessedness that on the fortieth day after his resurrection, after he had made careful provision for everything concerning the preaching of the gospel and the mysteries of the new covenant, our Lord Jesus Christ was taken up to heaven before the eyes of his disciples, and so his bodily presence among them came to an end. From that time onward he was to remain at the Father's right hand until the completion of the period ordained by God for the Church's children to increase and multiply, after which, in the same body with which he ascended, he will come again to judge the living and the dead.

And so our Redeemer's visible presence has passed into the sacraments. Our faith is nobler and stronger because sight has been replaced by a doctrine whose authority is accepted by believing hearts, enlightened from on high.

*(Sermon 74, 1-2: CCL 138A, 455-57)*

---

**Leo the Great** (c. 400-61) was elected pope in 440. At a time of general disorder he did much to strengthen the influence of the Roman see. Although he was not a profound theologian, Leo's teaching is clear and forceful. His Tome was accepted as a statement of Christological orthodoxy at the Council of Chalcedon (451). One hundred and forty-three of his letters and ninety-six sermons have survived. The latter, which cover the whole of the liturgical year, have been published in a critical edition.

# Seventh Sunday of Easter

*Gospel:* John 17:11-19

Father, may they all be one in us.

*Commentary:* Guerric of Igny

*Father, while I was with them I kept them in your name.* This was the prayer our Lord made on the eve of his passion. But it would not be inappropriate to apply it to the day of the ascension, when he was about to leave his disciples and entrust them to the Father. He who in heaven directs and governs the hosts of angels created by himself had chosen a small group of his disciples as his associates on earth. These he would instruct in person until the time when their hearts were sufficiently opened to be led by the Spirit. And so, great God that he was, Christ loved these little ones with a love worthy of his greatness. Having withdrawn them from secular pursuits, he knew they had abandoned all worldly ambitions and now relied on him alone. But as long as he shared their mortal way of life he did not lightly lavish on them marks of his affection; his manner toward them was grave rather than tender, as was fitting for a master and a father.

Now, however, when the moment was at hand for him to leave his disciples, he seemed overwhelmed by the depth of his affection for them, and unable to disguise the overflowing tenderness which until then he had hidden from them. Hence the words of the evangelist: *Having loved his own who were in the world, he loved them to the end.* He laid bare the whole strength of his love for his friends, before pouring himself out like water for his enemies. Handing over to them the sacrament of his body and blood, he instituted the celebration of the eucharist. It is hard to say which was the more wonderful, his power or his love, in devising this new means of remaining with them, to console them for his departure. In spite of the withdrawal of his bodily presence, he would remain not only with them but in them, by virtue of this sacrament.

62

It was at that moment that he commended them to his Father. Eyes raised to heaven, he said: *Father, while I was with them in the world, I kept them in your name, and none of them is lost but the son of perdition. And now I am coming to you. Keep those you have given me in your name. I do not pray that you should take them out of the world, but that you should keep them from the evil one.* Much more he went on to say; but the whole of his prayer can be summarized in these three petitions, which are themselves a summary of salvation, namely that the disciples should be kept from evil, sanctified in truth, and glorified with Christ.

*Father,* he said, *I desire that they too, whom you have given me, may be with me where I am, so that they may see my glory.* Happy those who have their judge for their advocate, pleading for them even while he must be adored with as much honor as the one to whom he addresses his prayers! The Father will not refuse the desire expressed by his lips, for he shares with him one single will and one single power, since God is one. All is bound to be accomplished that is requested by Christ, whose word is all-powerful and whose will is wholly efficacious. Of everything which exists, he spoke, and it was done; he commanded, and it stood forth. And now he says: *I desire that where I am, they too may be with me.*

What certainty for believers! Not to the apostles only, or to their companions, is this assurance offered, but to all those who through their word will believe in the Word of God: *I do not pray for these only, but also for those who through their word will believe in me.*

*(Sermon on the Ascension 1-2: PL 185, 153-55)*

---

**Guerric of Igny** (c. 1070/80-1157), about whose early life little is known, probably received his education at the cathedral school of Tournai, perhaps under the influence of Odo of Cambrai (1087-92). He seems to have lived a retired life of prayer and study near the cathedral of Tournai. He paid a visit to Clairvaux to consult Saint Bernard, and is mentioned by him as a novice in a letter to Ogerius in 1125/1256. He became abbot of the Cistercian abbey of Igny, in the diocese of Rheims in 1138. A collection of fifty-four authentic sermons preached on Sundays and feast days have been edited. Guerric's spirituality was influenced by Origen.

# Pentecost Sunday

*Gospel:* John 15:26-27; 16:12-15

As the Father sent me, so I send you: Receive the Holy Spirit.

*Commentary:* Aelred of Rievaulx

Today's holy solemnity puts new heart into us, for not only do we revere its dignity, we also experience it as delightful. On this feast it is love that we specially honor, and among human beings there is no word pleasanter to the ear, no thought more tenderly dwelt on, than love. The love we celebrate is nothing other than the goodness, kindness, and charity of God; for God himself is goodness, kindness, and charity. His goodness is identical with his Spirit, with God himself.

In his work of disposing all things *the Spirit of the Lord has filled the whole world* from the beginning, *reaching from end to end of the earth in strength, and delicately disposing everything;* but as sanctifier *the Spirit of the Lord has filled the whole world* since Pentecost, for on this day the gracious Spirit himself was sent by the Father and the Son on a new mission, in a new mode, by a new manifestation of his mighty power, for the sanctification of every creature. Before this day *the Spirit had not been given, for Jesus was not yet glorified,* but today he came forth from his heavenly throne to give himself in all his abundant riches to the human race, so that the divine outpouring might pervade the whole wide world and be manifested in a variety of spiritual endowments.

It is surely right that this overflowing delight should come down to us from heaven, since it was heaven that a few days earlier received from our fertile earth a fruit of wonderful sweetness. When has our land ever yielded a fruit more pleasant, sweeter, holier, or more delectable? Indeed, *faithfulness has sprung up from the earth.* A few days ago we sent Christ on ahead to the heavenly kingdom, so that in all fairness we might have in return whatever heaven held that should be sweet to our desire. The full sweetness of earth is Christ's humanity, the full sweetness of heaven Christ's Spirit. Thus a more profitable bargain was struck: Christ's human nature ascended from us to heaven, and on us today Christ's Spirit has come down.

Now indeed *the Spirit of the Lord has filled the whole earth,* and all creation recognizes his voice. Everywhere the Spirit is at work, everywhere he speaks. To be sure, the Holy Spirit was given to the disciples before our Lord's ascension when he said, *Receive the Holy Spirit: if you forgive anyone's sins they are forgiven; if you declare them unforgiven, unforgiven they remain;* but before the day of Pentecost the Spirit's voice was still in a sense unheard. His power had not yet leaped forth, nor had the disciples truly come to know him, for they were not yet confirmed by his might; they were still in the grip of fear, cowering behind closed doors.

From this day onward, however, *the voice of the Lord has resounded over the waters; the God of majesty has thundered and the Lord makes his voice echo over the flood.* From now on the *voice of the Lord speaks with strength, the voice of the Lord in majesty, the voice of the Lord fells the cedars, the voice of the Lord strikes flaring fire, the voice of the Lord shakes the desert, stirring the wilderness of Kadesh, the voice of the Lord strips the forest bare, and all will cry out, "Glory"!*

(*Talbot 1, 112-14*)

---

**Aelred of Rievaulx** (1109-67), a native of Yorkshire, spent part of his youth at the court of King David of Scotland. About the year 1133 he entered the Cistercian monastery of Rievaulx of which he later became abbot. His writings, which combine mystical and speculative theology, earned him the title, "The Bernard of the North." The most important works of this master of the spiritual life are *The Mirror of Charity* and *Spiritual Friendship.*

# Trinity Sunday

*Gospel:* Matthew 28:16-20

Baptize them in the name of the Father, and of the Son, and of the Holy Spirit.

*Commentary:* Nicholas Cabasilas

Although it was by a common benevolence that the Trinity saved our race, each one of the blessed persons played his own part. The Father was reconciled, the Son reconciled, and the Holy Spirit was the gift bestowed upon those who were now God's friends. The Father set us free, the Son was our ransom, and the Spirit our liberty, for Paul says, *Where the Spirit of the Lord is, there is liberty.* The Father recreated us through the Son, but *it is the Spirit who gives life.*

Even in the first creation there was a shadowy indication of the Trinity, for the Father created, the Son was the Creator's hand, and the Paraclete was the Life-giver's breath. But why speak of this? For in fact it is only in the new creation that the distinctions within the Godhead are revealed to us.

God bestowed many blessings on his creation in every age, but you will not find any of them being ascribed to the Father alone, or to the Son, or to the Spirit. On the contrary, all have their source in the Trinity, which performs every act by a single power, providence, and creativity. But in the dispensation by which the Trinity restored our race, something new occurred. It was still the Trinity that jointly willed my salvation, and providentially arranged the means for its accomplishment, but the Trinity no longer acted as one. The active role belonged not to the Father, or to the Spirit, but to the Word alone. It was the only-begotten Son alone who assumed flesh and blood, who was scourged, who suffered and died, and who rose again.

Through these acts of his our nature received new life; through these acts baptism was instituted—a new birth and a new creation. Only in this new creation are the distinctions within the Godhead revealed.

Therefore, when those who have obtained this holy re-creation call on God over the sacred bath, it is fitting that they should distinguish between the persons by invoking them as Father, Son, and Holy Spirit.

*(The Life of Christ 2: PG 150, 532-33)*

---

**Cabasilas, Nicholas** (b. 1322/23) was a native of Thessalonica. After receiving an excellent education, first at Thessalonica and then in Constantinople, he entered the imperial service, in which for ten years he played a prominent part. After the deposition in 1354 of his friend, the emperor John VI Cantacuzenos, Cabasilas entered the Manganon monastery near Constantinople, and probably became a priest. This was the period of his greatest literary output, his two principal works being *The Life in Christ* and *A Commentary on the Divine Liturgy,* both of which were written for lay people. The kernel of Cabasilas' teaching, which was praised by the Council of Trent and by Bossuet, is the Christians' deification by means of the sacraments. Cabasilas died some time after the capture of Thessalonica by the Turks in 1387.

# Corpus Christi

*Gospel:* Mark 14:12-16

This is my body. This is my blood.

*Commentary:* John Chrysostom

*As they were eating he took bread and broke it.* Christ instituted this sacrament at the time of the passover in order to teach us by every possible means both that he himself had been the lawgiver of the Old Testament, and also that the whole of the Old Testament had been a foreshadowing of these mysteries. He was replacing the type by the reality. The fact that it was evening signified that the fullness of time had come and that all was about to be accomplished. He gave thanks to teach us how we ought to celebrate these mysteries, to show that he was not going to his passion against his will, and to train us to accept with gratitude whatever we have to suffer and so to derive from it hope of future blessedness.

If the type was able to free a people from bondage, much more would the reality liberate the world, and Christ's death bring down blessings upon our race. We see then why he did not institute this sacrament before, but only when it was time to abolish the rites of the law. Christ put an end to the most important Jewish festival by offering his disciples another far more awe-inspiring meal. *Take, eat,* he said, *this is my body which is broken for many.* He told them that the reason he was going to suffer was to take away our sins. He spoke of the blood of the new covenant, that is of the promise, the new law. He had promised long before that the new covenant would be ratified by his blood. As the old covenant had been ratified by the blood of sheep and calves, so the new covenant was to be ratified by the blood of the Lord. Thus, by speaking of his covenant and by reminding them that the old covenant had also been inaugurated by the shedding of blood, he made known to them that he was soon to die. And he told them once again the reason for his death in the words, *This is my blood, which is poured out for all for the forgiveness of sins* and, *Do this in memory of me.*

Notice how he leads them away from the Jewish customs by saying, *Just as you used to do this in memory of the miracles performed in Egypt, so now you must do it in memory of me.* Blood was shed then for the salvation of the firstborn: It is to be shed now for the forgiveness of the sins of the whole world. *This*, he said, *is my blood, which is shed for the forgiveness of sins.* He said this to show that his passion and cross are a mystery, and so again to comfort his disciples. As Moses had said, *This shall be for you an everlasting memorial,* so now the Lord says, *"Do this in memory of me until I come."* This is why he also says, *I have longed to eat this passover,* meaning, "I have longed to hand over to you these new rites, and to give you the passover which will turn you into people moved by the Spirit."

*(Homilies on Matthew's Gospel 82, 1: PG 58, 737-39)*

**John Chrysostom** (c. 347-407) was born at Antioch and studied under Diodore of Tarsus, the leader of the Antiochene school of theology. After a period of great austerity as a hermit, he returned to Antioch where he was ordained deacon in 381 and priest in 386. From 386 to 397 it was his duty to preach in the principal church of the city, and his best homilies, which earned him the title "Chrysostomos" or "the golden-mouthed," were preached at this time. In 397 Chrysostom became patriarch of Constantinople, where his efforts to reform the court, clergy, and people led to his exile in 404 and finally to his death from the hardships imposed on him. Chrysostom stressed the divinity of Christ against the Arians and his full humanity against the Apollinarians, but he had no speculative bent. He was above all a pastor of souls, and was one of the most attractive personalities of the early Church.

# Sacred Heart

*Gospel:* John 19:31-37

One of the soldiers pierced his side with a lance, and immediately there came out blood and water.

*Commentary:* Catherine of Siena

"Why, gentle spotless Lamb, since you were dead when your side was opened, did you want your heart to be pierced and parted?"

He answered, "There were plenty of reasons, but I shall tell you one of the chief. My longing for humankind was infinite, but the actual deed of bearing pain and torment was finite and could never show all the love I had. This is why I wanted you to see my inmost heart, so that you would see that I loved you more than finite suffering could show.

"By shedding both blood and water I showed you the holy baptism of water that you receive through the power of my blood. But I was also showing you the baptism of blood, and this in two ways. The first touches those who are baptized in their own blood poured out for me. Though they could not have the other baptism, their own blood has power because of mine. Others are baptized in fire when they lovingly desire baptism but cannot have it. Nor is there any baptism of fire without blood, for blood has been fused with the fire of divine charity, because it was shed for love.

"There is a second way the soul receives this baptism of blood, figuratively speaking. This my divine charity provided because I know how people sin because of their weakness. Not that weakness or anything else can force them to sin if they do not want to, but being weak they do fall into deadly sin and lose the grace they had drawn from the power of the blood in holy baptism. So my divine charity had to leave them an ongoing baptism of blood accessible by heartfelt contrition and a holy confession as soon as they can confess to my ministers who hold the key to the blood. This blood the priest pours over the soul in absolution.

"So you see, this baptism is ongoing, and the soul ought to be baptized in it right up to the end, in the way I have told you. In this baptism you experience that though my act of suffering on the cross was finite, the fruit of that suffering which you have received through me is infinite. This is because of the infinite divine nature joined with finite human nature. It was this human nature in which I was clothed that suffered in me, the Word. But because the two natures are fused with each other, the eternal Divinity took to itself the suffering I bore with such burning love.

"For this reason what I did can be called infinite. Not that either the actual bodily suffering or the pain of my longing to accomplish your redemption was infinite, for all of that ended on the cross when my soul left my body. But the fruit was infinite that came from my suffering and from my desire for your salvation, and therefore you receive it without limit. Had it not been infinite, the whole of human-kind, past, present, and to come, would not have been restored. Nor could those who sin get up again if this baptism of blood (that is, the fruit of the blood) had not been given to you without limit.

"I showed you this in the opening up of my side. There you find my heart's secret and it shows you, more than any finite suffering could, how I love you."

*(The Dialogue 75, Classics of Western Spirituality, 138-39)*

---

**Catherine of Siena** (1347-80), Caterina di Giacomo di Benincasa, took a vow of virginity at the age of seven. At eighteen she received the Dominican habit, when she began to live in solitude and silence in her room. After her "mystical espousal" to Christ in 1368 she rejoined her family and devoted herself to the service of the poor and sick, but continued her life of contemplation during which she both learned and taught. In Pisa in 1373 she began her prolific letter-writing career. Through this, and her many travels, she sought to influence public affairs, and to bring about a reform of the clergy, and the return of the papacy to Rome from Avignon. Possessed of exceptional apostolic powers, especially in the reconciliation of sinners, she became the center of a group drawn from many levels of society and religious traditions, who regarded her as teacher and spiritual guide. As well as her *Dialogue*, a spiritual work of considerable importance, we still have many of Catherine's letters. She died in Rome at the age of 33, was canonized in 1461, and declared a doctor of the Church in 1970.

# Second Sunday in Ordinary Time

*Gospel:* John 1:35-42

They saw where Jesus lived, and they stayed with him.

*Commentary:* Basil of Seleucia

Spurred on by the testimony of John the Baptist, the glorious apostle Andrew left his teacher and ran to the one pointed out by him. John's words were his signal, and, moving more swiftly than John could speak, he approached the master with obvious longing, his companion, John the Evangelist, running beside him. Both had left the lamp to come to the sun.

Andrew was the first to become an apostle. It was he who opened the gates of Christ's teaching. He was the first to gather the fruits cultivated by the prophets, and he surpassed the hopes of all by being the first to embrace the one awaited by all. He was the first to show that the precepts of the law were in force only for a limited time. He was the first to restrain the tongue of Moses, for he would not allow it to speak after Christ had come. Yet he was not rebuked for this, because he did not dishonor the teacher of the Jews, but honored more the sender than the one sent. In fact Andrew was seen to be the first to honor Moses, because he was the first to recognize the one he foretold when he said: *The Lord God will raise up for you from among your kindred a prophet like myself. Listen to him.* Andrew set the law aside in obedience to the law. He listened to Moses who said: *Listen to him.* He listened to John who cried out: *Behold the Lamb of God,* and of his own accord went to the one pointed out to him.

Having recognized the prophet foretold by the prophets, Andrew led his brother to the one he had found. To Peter, who was still in ignorance, he revealed the treasure: *We have found the Messiah* for whom we were longing. How many sleepless nights we spent beside the waters of the Jordan, and now we have found the one for whom we longed! Nor was Peter slow when he heard these words, for he was Andrew's brother. He listened attentively, then hastened with great eagerness.

Taking Peter with him, Andrew brought his brother to the Lord, thus making him his fellow-disciple. This was Andrew's first achievement: he increased the number of the apostles by bringing Peter to Christ, so that Christ might find in him the disciples' leader. When later on Peter won approval, it was thanks to the seed sown by Andrew. But the commendation given to the one redounded to the other, for the virtues of each belonged to both, and each was proud of the other's merits. Indeed, when Peter promptly answered the master's question, how much joy he gave to all the disciples by breaking their embarrassed silence! Peter alone acted as the mouthpiece of those to whom the question was addressed. As though all spoke through him, he replied clearly on their behalf: *You are the Christ, the Son of the living God.* In one sentence he acknowledged both the Savior and his saving plan.

Notice how these words echo Andrew's. By prompting Peter the Father endorsed from above the words Andrew used when he led Peter to Christ. Andrew had said: *We have found the Messiah.* The Father said, prompting Peter: *You are the Christ, the Son of the living God,* almost forcing these words on Peter. "Peter," he said, "when you are questioned, use Andrew's words in reply. Show yourself very prompt in answering your master. Andrew did not lie to you when he said: *We have found the Messiah.* Turn the Hebrew words into Greek and cry out: *You are the Christ, the Son of the living God!*"

*(Exhortatory Sermon 3-4: PG 28, 1104-06)*

---

**Basil of Seleucia** (d. 459) became archbishop of Seleucia about the year 440. He is remembered for his fluctuating attitude in the events which preceded the Council of Chalcedon in 451. He voted against Monophysitism at the Synod of Constantinople in 448, but at the "Robber Synod" of Ephesus in 449 gave his support to Eutyches, the originator of Monophysitism. Then at the Council of Chalcedon he signed the Tome of Saint Leo, which condemned Eutyches. Thirty-nine of Basil's homilies have been preserved. They show his concern to place the exegesis of his time within the reach of all.

# Third Sunday
# in Ordinary Time

*Gospel:* Mark 1:14-20

Repent, and believe the good news.

*Commentary:* Caesarius of Arles

In today's gospel, beloved, we heard the exhortation to repent, for the kingdom of heaven is at hand. Now the kingdom of heaven is Christ, who, as we know, is the judge of good and evil and scrutinizes the motives for all our actions. We should therefore do well to forestall God's judgement by freely acknowledging our sins and correcting our wrongheaded attitudes; for by failing to seek out the needful remedies and apply them, we place ourselves in danger. And our knowledge that we shall have to account for the motives behind our shortcomings makes the need for such a change of heart even greater.

We must recognize the greatness of God's love for us; so generous is it that he is willing to be appeased by the amends we make for our evil deeds, provided only that we freely admit them before he has himself condemned them. And though his judgments are always just, he gives us a warning before he passes them, so as not to be compelled to apply the full rigor of his justice. It is not for nothing that our God draws floods of tears from us; he does so to incite us to recover by penance and a change of heart what we had previously let slip through carelessness. God is well aware that human judgment is often at fault, that we are prone to fleshly sins and deceitful speech. He therefore shows us the way of repentance, by which we can compensate for damage done and atone for our faults. And so to be sure of obtaining forgiveness, we ought to be always bewailing our guilt. Yet no matter how many wounds our human nature has sustained, we are never justified in giving ourselves over to despair, for the Lord is magnanimous enough to pour out his compassion abundantly on all who need it.

But perhaps one of you will say: "What have I to fear? I have never done anything wrong." On this point hear what the apostle John says: *If we claim to be sinless, we deceive ourselves and are blind to the truth.* So let no one lead you astray; the most pernicious kind of sin is the failure to realize one's own sinfulness. Once let wrongdoers admit their guilt and repent of it, and this change of heart will bring about their reconciliation with the Lord; but no sinner is more in need of the tears of others than the one who thinks he has nothing to weep for. So I implore you, beloved, to follow the advice given you by holy Scripture and *humble yourselves beneath the all-powerful hand of God.*

As none of us can be wholly free from sin, so let none of us fail to make amends; here too we do ourselves great harm if we presume our own innocence. It may be that some are less guilty than others, but no one is entirely free from fault; there may be degrees of guilt, but no one can escape it altogether. Let those then whose offenses are more grievous be more earnest in seeking pardon; and let those who have so far escaped contamination by the more heinous crimes pray that they may never be defiled by them, through the grace of our Lord Jesus Christ, who with the Father and the Holy Spirit lives and reigns for ever and ever. Amen.

*(Sermon 144, 1-4: CCL 104, 593-95)*

---

**Caesarius of Arles** (c. 470-543) was born in Chalon on the Saône. In 489 he entered as a monk at Lérins. He was so outstanding in the perfection of his life and in his sense of justice that he was eventually made archbishop of Arles. He legislated for both nuns and monks, his *Rule for Virgins* being written for his sister Saint Caesaria, superior of a community of nuns. Influenced by Saint Augustine's teaching on grace, he successfully combatted semi-Pelagianism at the Council of Orange in 529. He was a celebrated preacher; his practical charity was such that he melted down church plate to relieve prisoners, and the quality of his prayer is reflected in his challenging statement: "One worships that on which one's mind is intent during prayer."

# Fourth Sunday
# in Ordinary Time

*Gospel:* Mark 1:21-28

This is a new kind of teaching—he speaks with authority!

*Commentary:* John Henry Newman

At the time appointed Christ came forth from the Father and showed himself in this external world, first as its Creator, then as its teacher, the revealer of secrets, the mediator, the effluence of God's glory, and the express image of his person. Neither cloud nor image, emblem nor words, are interposed between the Son and his eternal Father. No language is needed between the Father and him, who is the very Word of the Father; no knowledge is imparted to him, who by his very nature and from eternity knows the Father and all that the Father knows. Such are his own words, *No one knows the Son but the Father, neither does anyone know the Father except the Son, and anyone to whom the Son chooses to reveal him.* Again he says, *Whoever has seen me has seen the Father;* and he accounts for this when he tells us that he and the Father are one, and that he is in the bosom of the Father and so can disclose him to humankind, as he was still in heaven, even while he was on earth.

Accordingly the blessed apostle draws a contrast between Moses and Christ to our comfort. *The Law,* he says, *was given by Moses, but grace and truth came by Jesus Christ.* In him God is fully and truly seen, so that he is absolutely the way, and the truth, and the life. All our duties are summed up for us in the message he brings us. Those who look towards him for teaching, who worship and obey him, will by degrees see *the light of the knowledge of the glory of God in* his *face,* and will be *changed into the same image from glory to glory.* And thus it happens that people of the lowest class and the humblest education may know fully the ways and works of God; fully, that is, as human beings can know them; far better and more truly than the most sagacious of this world from whom the gospel is hidden. Religion has a store of wonderful secrets which no one can communicate to another, and which are most pleasant and delightful to know. *Call on me,* says God by the prophet, *and I will answer you, and show you great and mighty things of which you have no knowledge.* This is no mere idle boast, but a fact which all who seek God will find to be true, though they cannot perhaps clearly express their meaning. Strange truths about ourselves, about God, about our duty, about the world, about heaven and hell, new modes of viewing things, discoveries which cannot be put into words, marvelous prospects and thoughts half understood, deep convictions inspiring joy and peace, these are a part of the revelation which Christ, the Son of God, brings to those who obey him. Moses had much toil to gain from the great God, some scattered rays of the truth, and that for his personal comfort, not for all Israel; but Christ has brought from his Father for all of us the full and perfect way of life. Thus he brings grace as well as truth, a most surprising miracle of mercy.

*(Parochial and Plain Sermons, 7, 124-6-modernized)*

---

**Newman, John Henry** (1801-90) was born in London and brought up in the Church of England. He went up to Trinity College, Oxford, in 1817, became a Fellow of Oriel five years later, was ordained deacon in 1824 and appointed Vicar of Saint Mary's, Oxford, in 1832. The impact of his sermons was tremendous. He was the leading spirit in the Tractarian Movement (1833-41) and the condemnation of Tract 90 led to his resignation from Saint Mary's in 1843. Two years later he was received into the Catholic Church. He was ordained in Rome and founded a house of Oratorians in Birmingham. Newman's *Essay on the Development Christian Doctrine* throws light on his withdrawal of previous objections to Roman Catholicism; his *Apologia* reveals the deepest motives underlying his outward attitudes, and the *Grammar of Assent* clarifies the subjective content of commitment to faith. In 1879 he was made a cardinal and he died at Edgbaston in 1890.

# Fifth Sunday
# in Ordinary Time

*Gospel:* Mark 1:29-39

He cured many who suffered from diseases of one kind or another.

*Commentary:* Peter Chrysologus

Those who have listened attentively to today's gospel will have learnt why the Lord of heaven, by whom all creation was renewed, entered the houses of his servants on earth. Nor should it surprise us that he so courteously adapted himself to every situation, since his motive in coming among us was to bring mercy and help to all.

You can easily see what drew Christ to Peter's house on this particular occasion; it was no desire to sit down and rest himself, but compassion for a woman stricken down by sickness. He was prompted not by the need to eat but by the opportunity to heal, his immediate preoccupation being the performance of a work which only his divine power could carry out, rather than the enjoyment of human company at table. In Peter's house that day it was not wine that flowed, but tears. Consequently Christ did not enter to obtain sustenance for himself, but to restore vitality to another. God wants human beings, not human goods. He desires to bestow what is heavenly, not to acquire anything earthly. Christ came to seek not our possessions but us.

As soon as Jesus crossed the threshold he saw Peter's mother-in-law lying ill in bed with a fever. On entering the house he immediately saw what he had come for. He was not interested in the comfort the house itself could offer, nor the crowds awaiting his arrival, nor the formal welcome prepared for him, nor the assembled household. Still less did he look for any outward signs of preparation for his reception. All he had eyes for was the spectacle of a sick woman, lying there consumed with a raging fever. At a glance he saw her desperate plight, and at once stretched out his hands to perform their divine work of healing; nor would he sit down to satisfy his human needs before he had made it possible for the stricken woman to rise up and serve her God. *So he took her by the hand, and the fever left her.* Here you see how fever loosens its grip on a person whose hand is held by Christ's; no sickness can stand its ground in the face of the very source of health. Where the Lord of life has entered, there is no room for death.

*(Sermon 18: PL 52, 246-49)*

Peter Chrysologus (c. 400-50), who was born at Imola in Italy, became bishop of Ravenna. He was highly esteemed by the Empress Galla Placidia, in whose presence he preached his first sermon as bishop. He was above all a pastor, and many of his sermons have been preserved.

# Sixth Sunday
# in Ordinary Time

*Gospel:* Mark 1:40-45

He sent the leper away, and he was cured.

*Commentary:* Paschasius Radbertus

However great our sinfulness, each one of us can be healed by God every day. We have only to worship him with humility and love, and wherever we are to say with faith: *Lord, if you want to you can make me clean. It is by believing from the heart that we are justified,* so we must make our petitions with the utmost confidence, and without the slightest doubt of God's power. If we pray with a faith springing from love, God's will need be in no doubt. He will be ready and able to save us by an all-powerful command. He immediately answered the leper's request, saying: *I do want to.* Indeed, no sooner had the leper begun to pray with faith than the Savior's hand began to cure him of his leprosy.

This leper is an excellent teacher of the right way to make petitions. He did not doubt the Lord's willingness through disbelief in his compassion, but neither did he take it for granted, for he knew the depths of his own sinfulness. Yet because he acknowledged that the Lord was able to cleanse him if he wished, we praise this declaration of firm faith just as we praise the Lord's mighty power. For obtaining a favor from God rightly depends as much on having a real living faith as on the exercise of the Creator's power and mercy. If faith is weak it must be strengthened, for only then will it succeed in obtaining health of body or soul. The Apostle's words, *purifying their hearts by faith* referred, surely, to strong faith like this. And so, if the hearts of believers are purified by faith, we must give thought to this virtue of faith, for, as the Apostle says, *Anyone who doubts is like a wave in the sea.*

A faith shown to be living by its love, steadfast by its perseverance, patient by its endurance of delay, humble by its confession, strong by its confidence, reverent by its way of presenting petitions, and discerning with regard to their content—such a faith may be certain that in every place it will hear the Lord saying: *I do want to.*

Pondering this wonderful reply, let us put the words together in their proper sequence. The leper began: *Lord, if you want to,* and the Savior said: *I do want to.* The leper continued: *You can make me clean,* and the Lord spoke his powerful word of command: *Be clean.* All that the sinner's true confession maintained with faith, love and power immediately conferred. And in case the gravity of his sins should make anyone despair, another Evangelist says this man who was cured had been completely covered with leprosy. For *all have sinned and forfeited the glory of God.* Since, as we rightly believe, God's power is operative everywhere, we ought to believe the same of his will. for *his will is that all should be saved and come to the knowledge of the truth.*

*(Commentary on Matthew's Gospel V, 8: PL 120, 341-42)*

**Paschasius Radbertus** (c. 785-860) was brought up by the nuns of Notre Dame at Soissons, after being left abandoned on their doorstep. He received the monastic habit at Corbie, and was the confidant of two successive abbots. On the death of Abbot Wala Paschasius himself became abbot, but he found the office uncongenial and resigned after seven years. He always refused to be raised to the priesthood. Paschasius, who was a prolific writer, is noted especially for the part he played in establishing the Catholic doctrine on the eucharist. He also wrote lengthy commentaries on Matthew and on the forty-fourth psalm.

# Seventh Sunday
# in Ordinary Time

*Gospel:* Mark 2:1-12

The Son of man has authority on earth to forgive sins.

*Commentary:* John Chrysostom

The scribes asserted that only God could forgive sins, yet Jesus not only forgave sins, but showed that he had also another power that belongs to God alone: the power to disclose the secrets of the heart. They, of course, did not reveal what they were thinking. Scripture says that *some of the scribes said within themselves: "This man is talking blasphemy." And Jesus, aware of their thoughts, said: "Why do you think evil in your hearts?"* Now only God knows the secrets of the heart. As the prophet says: *You alone know the heart,* and: *God searches the mind and the heart.* And so, to prove his divinity and his equality with the Father, Jesus brought their secret thoughts into the open, which they had not dared to do for fear of the crowds.

In doing this, he showed his great compassion. *Why do you think evil in your hearts?* he said. After all, if anyone had reason for complaint it was the invalid. As though cheated he might well have asked: "Have you come to heal something else then? To put right a different malady? How can I be sure that my sins are forgiven?" In fact, however, he said nothing of the sort, but surrendered himself to the healer's power.

The scribes, on the other hand, feeling left out and envious, plotted against the good of others. Jesus therefore rebuked them, but with forbearance. He said: "If you do not believe the first proof, and regard it as an empty boast, then see, I offer you another by revealing your secret thoughts; and to this I will add a third." What is the third to be? The healing of the paralytic.

Jesus did not give a clear manifestation of his power when he first spoke to the paralytic. He did not say: "I forgive you your sins," but: *Your sins are forgiven.* When the scribes forced him, however, he showed his power more ɔlearly, *that you may know,* he said, *that the Son of man has power on earth to forgive sins.*

Before doing this Jesus asked the scribes: *Which is easier to say, "Your sins are forgiven," or to say, "Pick up your mat and go home?"* This was the same as asking: "Which seems easier to you, to heal the body, or to forgive the soul its sins? Obviously, it is easier to heal the body. Indeed, as far as the soul is above the body, so far does the forgiveness of sins surpass physical healing. However, since the one is invisible, but the other visible, I grant you as well this lesser, visible miracle as proof of the one which is greater but invisible." Thus he showed by his deeds the truth of what John had said of him: that he takes away the sins of the world.

*(Homilies on Matthew's Gospel 29, 1: Bareille 12, 87-89)*

---

**John Chrysostom** (c. 347-407) was born at Antioch and studied under Diodore of Tarsus, the leader of the Antiochene school of theology. After a period of great austerity as a hermit, he returned to Antioch where he was ordained deacon in 381 and priest in 386. From 386 to 397 it was his duty to preach in the principal church of the city, and his best homilies, which earned him the title "Chrysostomos" or "the golden-mouthed," were preached at this time. In 397 Chrysostom became patriarch of Constantinople, where his efforts to reform the court, clergy, and people led to his exile in 404 and finally to his death from the hardships imposed on him. Chrysostom stressed the divinity of Christ against the Arians and his full humanity against the Apollinarians, but he had no speculative bent. He was above all a pastor of souls, and was one of the most attractive personalities of the early Church.

# Eighth Sunday
# in Ordinary Time

*Gospel:* Mark 2:18-22

The bridegroom is still with them.

*Commentary:* Paschasius Radbertus

A most strange, indeed, unheard of, marriage took place when, in the womb of the Virgin, *the Word became flesh and so dwelt among us.* Just as when Christ rose again all the elect rose again in him, so also this marriage was solemnized in Christ. The Church was joined to her bridegroom by a marriage covenant when the man-God received in their entirety the gifts of the Holy Spirit, and the fullness of the divine nature became embodied in him. The bride has already received as a marriage present a pledge from among these gifts, the gifts of the same Holy Spirit who dwelt fully in Christ, through whom he became man and like a bridegroom came forth from the womb of the Virgin, since her womb was his bridal chamber. When the Church is reborn of water in this same Spirit, she becomes one body in Christ, so that they are two in a single body. This is *a great mystery concerning Christ and the Church.*

This wedding lasts from the first moment of Christ's incarnation until his return, so that all its rites may be completed. Then those who are ready, having duly fulfilled the requirements of so exalted a marriage, will go in to the eternal wedding banquet with Christ, filled with awe. Meanwhile, Christ's promised bride is brought to her husband, and in faith and mercy they pledge themselves to one another every day until he comes again. This is what Paul said: *I have betrothed you to Christ to present you as a pure virgin to this one husband,* so that when Christ comes he may embrace the church, made up as it is of both Jews and Gentiles, as his bride, his consort, his spouse.

All the saints of the Old Testament, all who have lived since the beginning of the world and have believed in Christ's future coming to save the human race—all these shall share in this marriage feast which by faith they glimpsed from afar. As Scripture says: *He sent his servants to summon the invited guests to the marriage feast.* Those summoned had already received their invitation, since God had inspired them all, from the righteous Abel onward, to look forward to the coming of Christ.

*(Commentary on Matthew's Gospel X, 22: PL 120, 741-42)*

---

**Paschasius Radbertus** (c. 785-860) was brought up by the nuns of Notre Dame at Soissons, after being left abandoned on their doorstep. He received the monastic habit at Corbie, and was the confidant of two successive abbots. On the death of Abbot Wala Paschasius himself became abbot, but he found the office uncongenial and resigned after seven years. He always refused to be raised to the priesthood. Paschasius, who was a prolific writer, is noted especially for the part he played in establishing the Catholic doctrine on the eucharist. He also wrote lengthy commentaries on Matthew and on the forty-fourth psalm.

# Ninth Sunday
# in Ordinary Time

*Gospel:* Mark 2:23–3:6 or 2:23-28

The Son of man is master even of the Sabbath.

*Commentary:* Unknown Greek Author

Listen, my child, and I will tell you the reason why this tradition of observing the Lord's Day and refraining from work has been handed down to us. When our Lord gave the Sacrament to his disciples, he took bread and blessed it. Then he broke it and handed it to them saying: *Take, eat; this is my body, which is broken for you for the forgiveness of sins. In the same way he also gave the cup to them saying: Drink of this, all of you. This is my blood, the blood of the new covenant, which is poured out for you and for many for the forgiveness of sins. Do this, he said, in memory of me.*

Now this is the day we dedicate to the Lord's memory, so it is called the Lord's Day. Before the Lord's passion it was not called the Lord's Day, but the first day. On this day the Lord began the creation of the world, and on this day he gave the firstfruits of the resurrection to the world. This is the day on which, as we have said, he bade us celebrate the holy mysteries. This great day has therefore become for us the beginning of all graces. It was the beginning of the world's creation, the beginning of the resurrection, and it is the beginning of the week. Because of its three beginnings, this day signifies the primordial power of the holy Trinity.

Now every week has seven days. Six of these God has given to us for work, and one for prayer, rest, and making reparation for our sins, so that on the Lord's Day we may atone to God for any sins we have committed on the other six days.

Therefore, arrive early at the church of God; draw near to the Lord and confess your sins to him, repenting in prayer and with a contrite heart. Attend the holy and divine liturgy; finish your prayer and do not leave before the dismissal. Contemplate your master as he is broken and distributed, yet not consumed. If you have a clear conscience, go forward and partake of the body and blood of the Lord. But if your conscience condemns you for being guilty of wicked and immoral deeds, refrain from receiving communion until your conscience has been purified by repentance. Remain for the prayer, however, and do not leave the church until you are dismissed. Remember Judas, the traitor. Not remaining in prayer with all the others was the beginning of his downfall and destruction.

This day, as we have often said, was given to you for prayer and rest. *This is the day which the Lord has made; let us rejoice and be glad in it,* and give glory to him who rose on this day, together with the Father and the Holy Spirit, now, always, and for endless ages. Amen.

*(Sermon 6, 1-2. 6: PG 86/1, 416.421)*

# Tenth Sunday in Ordinary Time

*Gospel:* Mark 3:20-35

It is the end of Satan.

*Commentary:* Unknown Greek Author of the Fifth Century

The signs of the Lord's resurrection are obvious: deception has ceased, envy has been banished, strife is despised. Peace is held in honor, and war has been done away with. No longer do we bewail the Adam who was fashioned first; instead we glorify the second Adam. No longer do we reproach Eve for transgressing God's command: instead we bless Mary for being the Mother of God. No longer do we avert our eyes from the wood of the tree: instead we carry the Lord's cross. We no longer fear the serpent: instead we revere the Holy Spirit. We no longer descend into the earth: instead we reascend into heaven. We are no longer exiles from paradise: instead we live in Abraham's bosom. We no longer hear, "I have made your day like night": instead, inspired by the Holy Spirit, we sing: *This is the day which the Lord has made: let us keep it with gladness and rejoicing.* Why should we do so? Because the sun is no longer darkened: instead everything is bathed in light. Because the veil of the temple is no longer rent: instead the Church is recognized. Because we no longer hold palm branches: instead we carry the newly enlightened.

*This is the day which the Lord has made: let us keep it with gladness and rejoicing.* This is the day, this and no other, for there is only one queen, and not a throng of princesses. This is the day in the truest sense: the day of triumph, the day custom consecrates to the resurrection, the day on which we adorn ourselves with grace, the day on which we partake of the spiritual Lamb. This is the day on which milk is given to those born again, and on which God's plan for the poor is realized. *Let us keep it with gladness and rejoicing,* not by running off to the taverns, but by hastening to the martyrs' shrines; not by esteeming drunkenness, but by loving temperance; not by dancing in the marketplace, but by singing psalms at home. This day is a day of resurrection, not of revelry. No one can ascend to heaven dancing; no one in a state of drunkenness can attend upon a king. Let none of us, therefore, dishonor this day.

This is the day on which Adam was set free, and Eve delivered from her affliction. It is the day on which cruel death shuddered, the strength of hard stones was shattered and destroyed, the bars of tombs were broken and set aside. It is the day on which the bodies of people long dead were restored to their former life, and the laws of the underworld, hitherto ever powerful and immutable, were repealed. It is the day on which the heavens were opened at the rising of Christ the Lord, and on which, for the good of the human race, the flourishing and fruitful tree of the resurrection sent forth branches all over the world, as if the world were a garden. It is the day on which the lilies of the newly enlightened sprang up, the streams that sustained sinners ran dry, the strength of the devil drained away, and demonic armies were scattered.

*This,* then, *is the day which the Lord has made: let us keep it with gladness and rejoicing* by the grace of Christ. By his resurrection he has illuminated the whole world, which was *in darkness and in the shadow of death.* May glory and adoration be given to him together with the Father and the Holy Spirit for endless ages. Amen.

*(Easter Homilies 51, 1-3: SC 187, 318-22)*

# Eleventh Sunday in Ordinary Time

*Gospel:* Mark 4:26-34

The mustard seed grows into the biggest shrub of all.

*Commentary:* Peter Chrysologus

Brothers and sisters, you have heard today how the kingdom of heaven, for all its vastness, can be compared to a mustard seed: *the kingdom of heaven,* says the gospel, *is like a mustard seed.* A mustard seed! Is that the sum of believers' hopes? Is that what the faithful are longing for—a mustard seed, the blessed reward of virgins for their long years of self-restraint, the glorious prize won by martyrs at the cost of their blood? Is this the mystery no eye has seen, no ear heard, no human heart imagined; the mystery past telling that the Apostle assures us God has prepared for all who love him?

Let us not be too easily disappointed by our Lord's words. If we remember that *God's weakness is stronger than human strength, and God's foolishness wiser than human wisdom,* we shall find that this smallest seed of God's creation is greater than the whole wide world. It is up to us to sow this mustard seed in our minds and let it grow within us into a great tree of understanding reaching up to heaven and elevating all our faculties; then it will spread out branches of knowledge, the pungent savor of its fruit will make our mouths burn, its fiery kernel will kindle a blaze within us inflaming our hearts, and the taste of it will dispel our unenlightened repugnance. Yes, it is true: a mustard seed is indeed an image of the kingdom of God.

Christ is the kingdom of heaven. Sown like a mustard seed in the garden of the Virgin's womb, he grew up into the tree of the cross whose branches stretch across the world. Crushed in the mortar of the passion, its fruit has produced seasoning enough for the flavoring and preservation of every living creature with which it comes in contact.

As long as a mustard seed remains intact, its properties lie dormant; but when it is crushed they are exceedingly evident. So it was with Christ; he chose to have his body crushed, because he would not have his power concealed.

We too must crush this mustard see, in order to feel the force of this parable. Christ is king, because he is the source of all authority. Christ is the kingdom, because all the glory of his kingdom is within him. Christ is a man, because all humanity is restored in him. Christ is a mustard seed, because the infinitude of divine greatness is accommodated to the littleness of flesh and blood.

Do we need further examples? Christ became all things in order to restore all of us in himself. The man Christ received the mustard seed which represents the kingdom of God; as man he received it, though as God he had always possessed it. He sowed it in his garden, that is in his bride, the Church. The Church is a garden extending over the whole world, tilled by the plough of the gospel, fenced in by stakes of doctrine and discipline, cleared of every harmful weed by the labor of the apostles, fragrant and lovely with perennial flowers: virgins' lilies and martyrs' roses set amid the pleasant verdure of all who bear witness to Christ and the tender plants of all who have faith in him.

Such then is the mustard seed which Christ sowed in his garden. When he promised a kingdom to the partriarchs the seed took root in them; with the prophets it sprang up, with the apostles it grew tall, in the Church it became a great tree putting forth innumerable branches laden with gifts. And now you too must take the wings of the psalmist's dove, gleaming gold in the rays of divine sunlight, and fly to rest for ever among those sturdy, fruitful branches. No snares are set to trap you there; fly off, then, with confidence and dwell securely in its shelter.

*(Sermon 98: PL 52, 474-76)*

---

**Peter Chrysologus** (c. 400-50), who was born at Imoly in Italy, became a bishop of Ravenna. He was highly esteemed by the Empress Galla Placidia, in whose presence he preached his first sermon as bishop. He was above all a pastor, and many of his sermons have been preserved.

# Twelfth Sunday
# in Ordinary Time

*Gospel:* Mark 4:35-41

Who can this be? Even the wind and the sea obey him.

*Commentary:* Augustine

With the Lord's help I want to speak to you about today's reading from the holy gospel, and to urge you in his name not to let your faith lie dormant in your hearts when you are buffeted by the winds and waves of this world. The Lord Christ's power is by no means dead, nor is it asleep. Do you think the Almighty was overcome by sleep in the boat against his will? If you do, then Christ is asleep in your hearts. If he were indeed keeping watch within you, then your faith too would be vigilant. The Apostle, remember, speaks of Christ dwelling in your hearts through faith.

This sleep of Christ has a symbolic meaning. The boat's crew are human souls sailing across the sea of this world in a wooden vessel. That vessel, of course, also represents the Church; but as each one of us is a temple of God, each one's heart is a sailing boat, nor can it be wrecked so long as we fill our minds only with what is good.

When you have to listen to abuse, that means you are being buffeted by the wind; when your anger is roused, you are being tossed by the waves. So when the winds blow and the waves mount high, the boat is in danger, your heart is imperiled, your heart is taking a battering. On hearing yourself insulted, you long to retaliate; but the joy of revenge brings with it another kind of misfortune—shipwreck. Why is this? Because Christ is asleep in you. What do I mean? I mean you have forgotten his presence. Rouse him, then; remember him, let him keep watch within you, pay heed to him. Now what was your desire? You wanted to get your own back. You have forgotten that when Christ was being crucified he said: *Father, forgive them, for they know not what they do.* Christ, the sleeper in your heart, had no desire for vengeance in his. Rouse him, then, call him to mind. (To remember him is to recall his words; to remember him is to recall his commands.) Then, when he is awake within you, you will ask yourself, "Whatever kind of wretch am I to be thirsting for revenge? Who am I to threaten another? Suppose I were to die before I were avenged! Suppose I were to take leave of my body breathing out threats, inflamed with rage and thirsting for that vengeance which Christ himself never sought; would he not refuse to receive me? He who said, *Give and it shall be given you; forgive and you will be forgiven,* would indeed decline to acknowledge me. So I will curb my anger and restore peace to my heart."

Now all is calm again. Christ has rebuked the sea. What I have said about anger must be your rule of conduct in every temptation. A temptation arises: it is the wind. It disturbs you: it is the surging of the sea. This is the moment to awaken Christ and let him remind you of those words: *Who can this be? Even the winds and the sea obey him.* Who is this whom the sea obeys? It is he to whom the sea belongs, for he made it; all things were made through him.

Try, then, to be more like the wind and the sea; obey the God who made you. The sea obeys Christ's command, and are you going to turn a deaf ear to it? The sea obeys him, the wind is still; will you persist with your blustering? Words, actions, schemes, what are all these but a constant huffing and puffing, a refusal to be still at Christ's command?

When your heart is in this troubled state, do not let the waves overwhelm you. If, since we are only human, the driving wind should stir up in us a tumult of emotions, let us not despair but awaken Christ, so that we may sail in quiet waters, and at last reach our heavenly homeland.

*(Sermon 63, 1-3: PL 38, 424-25)*

---

**Augustine** (354-430) was born at Thagaste in Africa and received a Christian education, although he was not baptized until 387. In 391 he was ordained priest and in 395 he became coadjutor bishop to Valerius of Hippo, whom he succeeded in 396. Augustine's theology was formulated in the course of his struggle with three heresies: Manichaeism, Donatism, and Pelagianism. His writings are voluminous and his influence on subsequent theology immense. He molded the thought of the Middle Ages down to the thirteenth century. Yet he was above all a pastor and a great spiritual writer.

# Thirteenth Sunday in Ordinary Time

*Gospel:* Mark 5:21-43 or 5:21-24.35-43

Little girl, I say to you, arise.

*Commentary:* Peter Chrysologus

Every gospel reading, beloved, is most helpful both for our present life and for the attainment of the life to come. Today's reading, however, sums up the whole of our hope, banishing all grounds for despair.

Let us consider the synagogue official who took Christ to his daughter and in so doing gave the woman with a hemorrhage an opportunity to approach him. Here is the beginning of today's reading: An official came to Jesus and did homage, saying: *Lord, my little daughter has just died, but come and lay your hand on her and she will live.*

Christ could foresee the future and he knew this woman would approach him. Through her the Jewish official was to learn that there is no need to move God to another place, take him on a journey, or attract him by a physical presence. One must only believe that he is present in the whole of his being always and everywhere, and that he can do all things effortlessly by a simple command; that far from depriving us of strength, he gives it; that he puts death to flight by a word of command rather than by physical touch, and gives life by his mere bidding, without need of any art.

*My daughter has just died. Do come.* What he means is that the warmth of life still remains, there are still indications that her soul has not departed, her spirit is still in this world, the head of the house still has a daughter, the underworld is still unaware of her death. Come quickly and hold back the departing soul!

In his ignorance the man assumed that Christ would not be able to raise his daughter unless he actually laid his hand on her. So when Christ reached the house and saw the mourners lamenting as though the girl were dead, he declared that she was not dead but sleeping, in order to move their unbelieving minds to faith and convince them that one can rise from death more easily than from sleep. *The girl is not dead,* he told them, *but asleep.* And indeed, for God death is nothing but sleep. He can restore life-giving warmth to limbs grown cold in death sooner than we can impart vigor to bodies sunk in slumber. Listen to the Apostle: *In an instant, in the twinkling of an eye, the dead will rise.* He used an image because it was impossible to express the speed of the resurrection in words. How could he explain its swiftness verbally when divine power outstrips the very notion of swiftness? How could time enter the picture when an eternal gift is given outside of time? Time implies duration, but eternity excludes time.

*(Sermon 34: PL 52, 296-99)*

---

**Peter Chrysologus** (c. 400-50), who was born at Imoly in Italy, became a bishop of Ravenna. He was highly esteemed by the Empress Galla Placidia, in whose presence he preached his first sermon as bishop. He was above all a pastor, and many of his sermons have been preserved.

# Fourteenth Sunday in Ordinary Time

*Gospel:* Mark 6:1-6

A prophet is despised only in his own country.

*Commentary:* Symeon the New Theologian

Brothers and Fathers, many people never stop saying—I have heard them myself—"If only we had lived in the days of the apostles, and been counted worthy to gaze upon Christ as they did, we should have become holy like them." Such people do not realize that the Christ who spoke then and the Christ who speaks now throughout the whole world is one and the same. If he were not the same then and now, God in every respect, in his operations as in the sacraments, how would it be seen that the Father is always in the Son and the Son in the Father, according to the words Christ spoke through the Spirit: *My Father is still working and so am I?*

But no doubt someone will say that merely to hear his words now and to be taught about him and his kingdom is not the same thing as to have seen him then in the body. And I answer that indeed the position now is not the same as it was then, but our situation now, in the present day, is very much better. It leads us more easily to a deeper faith and conviction than seeing and hearing him in the flesh would have done.

Then he appeared to the uncomprehending Jews as a man of lowly station: now he is proclaimed to us as true God. Then in his body he associated with tax collectors and sinners and ate with them: now he is seated at the right hand of God the Father, and is never in any way separated from him. We are firmly persuaded that it is he who feeds the entire world, and we declare—at least if we are believers—that without him nothing came into being. Then even those of lowliest condition held him in contempt. They said: *Is not this the son of Mary, and of Joseph the carpenter?* Now kings and rulers worship him as Son of the true God, and himself true God, and he has glorified and continues to glorify those who worship him in spirit and in truth, although he often punishes them when they sin. He transforms them, more than all the nations under heaven, from clay into iron. Then he was thought to be mortal and corruptible like the rest of humankind. He was no different in appearance from other men. The formless and invisible God, without change or alteration, assumed a human form and showed himself to be a normal human being. He ate, he drank, he slept, he sweated, and he grew weary. He did everything other people do, except that he did not sin. For anyone to recognize him in that human body, and to believe that he was the God who made heaven and earth and everything in them was very exceptional.

This is why when Peter said: *You are the Son of the living God,* the master called him blessed, saying: *Blessed are you, Simon Bar-Jonah, for flesh and blood has not revealed this to you*—you do not speak of something your eyes have seen—*but my Father who is in heaven.*

It is certain therefore that anyone who now hears Christ cry out daily through the holy Gospels, and proclaim the will of his blessed Father, but does not obey him with fear and trembling and keep his commandments—it is certain that such a person would have refused to believe in him then, if he had been present, and seen him, and heard him teach. Indeed there is reason to fear that in his total incredulity he would have blasphemed by regarding Christ not as true God, but as an enemy of God.

*(Catechesis III, 19: SC 113, 165-69)*

---

**Symeon the New Theologian** (949-1022) was born in Galata in Paphlagonia, and educated in Constantinople, where in 977 he entered the famous monastery of Studios. Soon afterward he transferred to the nearby monastery of Saint Mamas, was ordained priest in 980, and about three years later became abbot. During his twenty-five years of office he instilled a new fervor into his community, but opposition to his teaching forced him to resign in 1005 and in 1009 he was exiled to Palonkiton on the other side of the Bosphorus. He turned the ruined oratory of Saint Marina into another monastery, and although he was soon pardoned, chose to remain there until his death rather than compromise his teaching.

# Fifteenth Sunday
# in Ordinary Time

*Gospel:* Mark 6:7-13

He called the twelve, and began to send them out.

*Commentary:* Theophylact

Besides teaching himself the Lord also sent out the Twelve in pairs. The reason for sending them in pairs was so that they would go more readily, for they might not have been so willing to set out all alone, and, on the other hand, if he had sent more than two together, there would not have been enough apostles to cover all the villages. So he sent them two by two: *two are better than one,* as Ecclesiastes says.

He commanded them to take nothing with them, neither bag, nor money, nor bread, so as to teach them to despise riches, and to make people ashamed when they saw them preaching poverty by their own lack of possessions. For who would not blush for shame, strip himself of his possessions, and embrace a life of poverty when he saw an apostle carrying neither bag, nor even bread which is so very essential?

The Lord instructed them to stay in the same house so as not to give the appearance of restlessness, as though they moved from one family to another in order to satisfy their stomachs. On the other hand, he told them to shake the dust off their feet when people refused to receive them, to show that they had made a long journey for their sakes and they owed them nothing; they had received nothing from them, not even their dust, which they shook off as a testimony against them—a testimony of reproach. *Be sure of this, I tell you: Sodom and Gomorrah will fare better on the Day of Judgment* than those who will not receive you. The Sodomites were punished in this world, so they will be punished less severely in the next. What is more, no apostles were sent to them. For those who refused to receive the apostles greater sufferings are in store.

*So they set out to preach repentance. They cast out many demons, and anointed many sick people with oil and cured them.* The fact that the apostles anointed the sick with oil is mentioned only by Mark, but the practice is also referred to in his general letter by James, the brother of the Lord, who says: *Are there any sick people among you? Let them send for the elders of the Church and let these pray over them, anointing them with oil.* Oil is beneficial for the relief of suffering, and it also produces light and makes for cheerfulness. It symbolizes the mercy of God and the grace of the Spirit, through which we are freed from suffering and receive light, gladness, and spiritual joy.

*(Commentary on Mark's Gospel: PG 123, 548-49)*

---

**Theophylact** (c. 1050-1109), theologian and language scholar, studied at Constantinople. He taught rhetoric and was tutor to the imperial heir presumptive: hence his treatise on the *Education of Monarchs.* In 1078 he became archbishop of Ochrida in Bulgarian territory. While diffusing Byzantine culture among the Slavs, he allowed the use of Slavonic texts. He wrote commentaries on several books of the Old Testament and all of the New except Revelation. He especially stressed practical morality, as did Chrysostom, his model.

# Sixteenth Sunday in Ordinary Time

*Gospel:* Mark 6:30-34

They were like sheep without a shepherd.

*Commentary:* Bede

*The apostles returned to Jesus and reported to him everything they had done and taught.* As well as reporting to him what they themselves had done and taught, they told him what had befallen John the Baptist while they were teaching. And he said to them: *Come away to some place where you can be alone by yourselves and rest awhile.*

The following words show what real need there was to give the disciples some rest: *For many were coming and going and they had no time even to eat.* The great happiness of those days can be seen from the hard work of those who taught and the enthusiasm of those who learned. If only in our time such a concourse of faithful listeners would again press round the ministers of the word, not allowing them time to attend to their physical needs! For those denied the time needed to look after their bodies will have still less opportunity to heed the soul's or the body's temptations. Rather, people of whom the word of faith and the saving ministry is demanded in season and out of season have an incentive to meditate upon heavenly things so as not to contradict what they teach by what they do.

*And they got into the boat and went away by themselves to a deserted spot.* The disciples did not get into the boat alone, but took the Lord with them, as the evangelist Matthew makes clear.

*Many people saw them set out and recognized them, and from all the towns they hastened to the place on foot and reached it before them.* The fact that people on foot are said to have reached the place first shows that the disciples did not go with our Lord to the opposite bank of the sea or the Jordan, but crossed some stream or inlet to reach a nearby spot in the same region, within walking distance for the local people.

*Thus when Jesus landed he saw a large crowd. He took pity on them because they were like sheep without a shepherd; and he began to teach them many things.*

Matthew relates more fully how he took pity on them. He says: *And he took pity on them and cured their sick.* This is what it means really to take pity on the poor, and on those who have no one to guide them: to open the way of truth to them by teaching, to heal their physical infirmities, and to make them want to praise the divine generosity by feeding them when they are hungry as Jesus did according to the following verses.

Jesus tested the crowd's faith, and having done so he gave it a fitting reward. He sought out a lonely place to see if they would take the trouble to follow him. For their part, they showed how concerned they were for their salvation by the effort they made in going along the deserted road not on donkeys or in carts of various kinds, but on foot. In return Jesus welcomed those weary, ignorant, sick, and hungry people, instructing, healing, and feeding them as a kindly savior and physician, and so letting them know how pleased he is by believers' devotion to him.

*(Commentary on Mark's Gospel: CCL 120, 510-11)*

---

**Bede** (c. 673-735), who received the title of Venerable less than a century after his death, was placed at the age of seven in the monastery of Wearmouth, then ruled by Saint Benet Biscop. From there he was sent to Jarrow, probably at the time of its foundation in about 681. At the age of thirty he was ordained priest. His whole life was devoted to the study of Scripture, to teaching, ﹒ﾠing, and the prayer of the Divine Office. He was famous for his learning, although he never went beyond the bounds of his native Northumbria. Bede is best known for his historical works, which earned him the title "Father of English History." His *Historia Ecclesiastica Gentis Anglorum* is a primary source for early English history, especially valuable because of the care he took to give his authorities, and to separate historical fact from hearsay and tradition. In 1899 Bede was proclaimed a doctor of the Church.

# Seventeenth Sunday in Ordinary Time

*Gospel:* John 6:1-15

He distributed to those who were seated as much as they wanted.

*Commentary:* Augustine

The miracles wrought by our Lord Jesus Christ are truly divine works, which lead the human mind through visible things to a perception of the Godhead. God is not the kind of being that can be seen with the eyes, and small account is taken of the miracles by which he rules the entire universe and governs all creation because they recur so regularly. Scarcely anyone bothers to consider God's marvelous, his amazing artistry in every tiny seed. And so certain works are excluded from the ordinary course of nature, works which God in his mercy has reserved for himself, so as to perform them at appropriate times. People who hold cheap what they see every day are dumbfounded at the sight of extraordinary works even though they are no more wonderful than the others.

Governing the entire universe is a greater miracle than feeding five thousand people with five loaves of bread, yet no one marvels at it. People marvel at the feeding of the five thousand not because this miracle is greater, but because it is out of the ordinary.

Who is even now providing nourishment for the whole world if not the God who creates a field of wheat from a few seeds? Christ did what God does. Just as God multiplies a few seeds into a whole field of wheat, so Christ multiplied the five loaves in his hands. For there was power in the hands of Christ. Those five loaves were like seeds, not because they were cast on the earth but because they were multiplied by the one who made the earth.

This miracle was presented to our senses in order to stimulate our minds; it was put before our eyes in order to engage our understanding, and so make us marvel at the God we do not see because of his works which we do see. For then, when we have been raised to the level of faith and purified by faith, we shall long to behold, though not with our eyes, the invisible God whom we recognize through what is visible.

This miracle was performed for the multitude to see; it was recorded for us to hear. Faith does for us what sight did for them. We behold with the mind what our eyes cannot see; and we are preferred to them because of us it was said: *Blessed are those who have not seen and yet believe.*

*When the people saw the sign Jesus had performed they said: Surely this must be a prophet.* He was in fact the Lord of the prophets, the fulfiller of the prophets, the sanctifier of the prophets; yet he was still a prophet, for Moses had been told: *I will raise up for them a prophet like yourself.* The Lord is a prophet, and the Lord is the Word of God, and without the Word of God no prophet can prophesy. The Word of God is with the prophets, and the Word of God is a prophet. People of former times were deemed worthy to have prophets inspired and filled by the Word of God; we have been deemed worthy to have as our prophet the Word of God himself.

(*Homilies on the Gospel of John 24, 1.6.7: CCL 36, 244.247-48*)

---

**Augustine** (354-430) was born at Thagaste in Africa and received a Christian education, although he was not baptized until 387. In 391 he was ordained priest and in 395 he became coadjutor bishop to Valerius of Hippo, whom he succeeded in 396. Augustine's theology was formulated in the course of his struggle with three heresies: Manichaeism, Donatism, and Pelagianism. His writings are voluminous and his influence on subsequent theology immense. He molded the thought of the Middle Ages down to the thirteenth century. Yet he was above all a pastor and a great spiritual writer.

# Eighteenth Sunday
# in Ordinary Time

*Gospel:* John 6:24-35

Whoever comes to me will never be hungry; whoever believes in me will never thirst.

*Commentary:* Theophylact

O*ur ancestors ate manna in the desert; as it is written, "He gave them bread from heaven to eat."* Wishing to persuade Christ to perform the kind of miracle that would provide them with bodily nourishment, the people in their insatiable greed called to mind the manna. What was the reply of our Lord Jesus, the infinite wisdom of God? *It was not Moses who gave you bread.* In other words, "Moses did not give you the true bread. On the contrary, everything that happened in his time was a prefiguration of what is happening now. Moses represented God, the real leader of the spiritual Israelites, while that bread typified myself, who have come down from heaven and who am the true bread which gives genuine nourishment." Our Lord refers to himself as the true bread not because the manna was something illusory, but because it was only a type and a shadow, and not the reality it signified.

This bread, being the Son of the living Father, is life by its very nature, and accordingly gives life to all. Just as earthly bread sustains the frail substance of the flesh and prevents it from falling into decay, so Christ quickens the soul through the power of the Spirit, and also preserves even the body for immortality. Through Christ resurrection from the dead and bodily immortality have been gratuitously bestowed upon the human race.

*Jesus said to the people: "I am the bread of life. Whoever comes to me shall never hunger, and whoever believes in me shall never thirst."* He did not say "the bread of bodily nourishment," but "the bread of life." For when everything had been reduced to a condition of spiritual death, the Lord gave us life through himself, who is bread because, as we believe, the leaven in the dough of our humanity was baked through and through by the fire of his divinity. He is the bread not of this ordinary life, but of a very different kind of life which death will never cut short.

Whoever believes in this bread will never hunger, will never be famished for want of hearing the Word of God; nor will such a person be parched by spiritual thirst through lack of the waters of baptism and the consecration imparted by the Spirit. The unbaptized, deprived of the refreshment afforded by the sacred water, suffer thirst and great aridity. The baptized, on the other hand, being possessed of the Spirit, enjoy its continual consolation.

*(Commentary on John's Gospel: PG 123, 1297-1301)*

**Theophylact** (c. 1050-1109), theologian and language scholar, studied at Constantinople. He taught rhetoric and was tutor to the imperial heir presumptive: hence his treatise on the *Education of Monarchs*. In 1078 he became archbishop of Ochrida in Bulgarian territory. While diffusing Byzantine culture among the Slavs, he allowed the use of Slavonic texts. He wrote commentaries on several books of the Old Testament and all of the New except Revelation. He especially stressed practical morality, as did Chrysostom, his model.

# Nineteenth Sunday in Ordinary Time

*Gospel:* John 6:41-51

I am the living bread that came down from heaven.

*Commentary:* Attributed to Denis the Areopagite

In his goodness and love for humankind, Jesus, the most divine Word, one, simple, and hidden, assumed our nature, appearing though unchanged in his own nature as a being both composite and visible. Graciously he received us into unifying communion with himself, joining our lowliness to his sublime divinity, upon the sole condition that we in our turn should adhere to him as members of his body by living a pure and godly life like his, and not giving reign to ruinous, death-dealing passions, which would make us incapable of union with those completely healthy and divine members.

If we aspire to communion with Jesus, we must fix our eyes upon the most holy life he lived in the flesh and follow the example of his divine innocence so as to become pure and godlike. Then, in a manner befitting us, he will give us a resemblance to himself.

The bishop manifests these truths in the sacred rites he performs when he publicly unveils the hidden gifts, divides them into many parts, and by the perfect union of the sacrament he distributes with those who receive it, admits the recipients to communion with it. For by thus presenting Jesus Christ to our eyes he shows us the very life of our spirit and understanding in a way perceptible to our senses, as it were pictorially. He shows us how Christ came forth from his divine concealment to assume for love of humanity our human form, becoming completely human without loss of his own identity; how while remaining unchanged he descended from his natural unity to the level of our divisibility; and how through the beneficent deeds inspired by his love for us, he calls the human race to communion with himself and to a share in his blessings. He asks only that we unite ourselves to his most divine life by imitating it to the best of our ability, so as to enter into a real communion with God and his divine mysteries.

*(The Ecclesiastical Hierarchy: PG 3, 444)*

---

**Denis the Areopagite**, Pseudo, was a mystical theologian who wrote approximately between the years 480 and 510, probably in Syria. The fictitious attribution of his writings to Denis of Athens greatly increased his influence. In the sixteenth century this identification was called in question and at the beginning of the twentieth century his doctrinal orthodoxy also was attacked. Recently however a more balanced judgement has prevailed. Careful examination of the philosophy underlying his spiritual doctrine has proved the validity of his teaching on the apophatic approach to God in prayer, characteristic also of the Cloud of Unknowing and the doctrine of Saint John of the Cross. The writings of Pseudo-Denis consist of the Celestial Hierarchy, the Ecclesiastical Hierarchy, the Divine Names, and about ten letters.

# Twentieth Sunday in Ordinary Time

*Gospel:* John 6:51-58

My flesh is real food, and my blood is real drink.

*Commentary:* Theophylact

We have heard that unless we eat the flesh of the Son we shall not have life. We must have unwavering faith, then, when we partake of the sacred mysteries, and not inquire "How?" Unspiritual people, that is, those led by a natural, human way of thinking, are not open to spiritual realities surpassing the natural order, and so lack understanding of the spiritual nourishment the Lord's flesh affords.

Those who do not share in this flesh will not share in eternal life because they reject Jesus, the true life. What is consumed is the flesh not of a mere man but of God, and being one with the Godhead, it has power to deify. This is real nourishment: its sustaining power does not last only for a time; it does not decompose like perishable food, but helps us to attain everlasting life. Likewise the cup of the Lord's blood is real drink, for it does not quench our thirst only for a time, but keeps those who drink it free from thirst for ever; as the Lord said to the Samaritan woman: *Whoever drinks of the water that I shall give will never thirst again.* Whoever receives the grace of the Holy Spirit by sharing in the divine mysteries will never suffer from spiritual hunger and thirst the way unbelievers do.

*Those who eat my flesh and drink my blood live in me, and I live in them. As I draw life from the living Father who sent me, so whoever eats me will draw life from me.* From these words we can begin to understand the mystery of communion. Those who eat and drink the Lord's flesh and blood live in the Lord and the Lord lives in them. A marvelous and inexplicable union occurs by which God is in us, and we are in God. Does this not fill you with awe as you listen?

It is not God alone that we eat, for he is intangible and incorporeal; he can be apprehended neither by our eyes nor by our teeth; nor, on the other hand, is it simply the flesh of a man, which would avail us nothing. Rather, in a union defying explanation, God has made flesh one with himself, so that the flesh now has life-giving power. This is not because its nature is changed into the nature of God. Of course not! A comparison may be made with iron put into fire. It remains iron but displays the energy of fire. So also the Lord's flesh remains flesh, but it has life-giving power because it is the flesh of the Word of God.

And so Christ says: *As I draw life from the Father,* or in other words, As I was born of the Father who is life, *so those who eat me will draw life from me,* because they will be united to me and as it were transformed into me, who am possessed of life-giving power.

*(Commentary on John's Gospel: PG 123, 1309-12)*

---

**Theophylact** (c. 1050-1109), theologian and language scholar, studied at Constantinople. He taught rhetoric and was tutor to the imperial heir presumptive: hence his treatise on the *Education of Monarchs*. In 1078 he became archbishop of Ochrida in Bulgarian territory. While diffusing Byzantine culture among the Slavs, he allowed the use of Slavonic texts. He wrote commentaries on several books of the Old Testament and all of the New except Revelation. He especially stressed practical morality, as did Chrysostom, his model.

# Twenty-First Sunday in Ordinary Time

*Gospel:* John 6:60-69

Lord, to whom shall we go? You have the words of eternal life.

## *Commentary:* Cyril of Alexandria

*To whom shall we go?* Peter asks. In other words, "Who else will instruct us the way you do?" or, "To whom shall we go to find anything better?" *You have the words of eternal life;* not hard words, as those other disciples say, but words that will bring us to the loftiest goal, unceasing, endless life removed from all corruption. These words surely make quite obvious to us the necessity for sitting at the feet of Christ, taking him as our one and only teacher, and giving him our constant and undivided attention. He must be our guide who knows well how to lead us to everlasting life. Thus, shall we ascend to the divine court of heaven, and entering the church of the first born, delight in blessings passing all human understanding.

That the desire to follow Christ alone and to be with him always is a good thing leading to our salvation is entirely self-evident; yet we may learn this from the Old Testament as well. When the Israelites had shaken off Egyptian tyranny and were hastening toward the promised land, God did not allow them to make disorderly marches; nor did the lawgiver let each one go where he would, for without a guide they should undoubtedly have lost the way completely. They were ordered to follow: to set out with the cloud, to come to a halt again with it, and to rest with it. Keeping with their guide was the Israelites' salvation then, just as not leaving Christ is ours now. For he was with those people of old under the form of the tabernacle, the cloud, and the fire.

They were commanded to follow, and not undertake the journey on their own initiative. They were to halt with the cloud and to abide with

110

it, that by this symbol you might understand Christ's words: *Whoever serves me must follow me, so as to be with me wherever I am.* For being always in his company means being steadfast in following him and constant in cleaving to him. But accompanying the Savior Christ and following him is by no means to be thought of as something done by the body. It is accomplished rather by deeds springing from virtue. Upon such virtue the wisest disciples firmly fixed their minds and refused to depart with the unbelievers, which they saw would be fatal. With good reason they cried out, "Where can we go?" It was as though they said: "We will stay with you always and hold fast to your commandments. We will receive your words without finding fault or thinking your teaching hard as the ignorant do, but thinking rather, *How sweet are your words to my throat! Sweeter to my mouth are they than honey or the honeycomb.*"

*(Commentary on John's Gospel IV, 4: PG 73, 613-17)*

---

**Cyril of Alexandria** (d. 444) succeeded his uncle Theophilus as patriarch in 412. Until 428 the pen of this brilliant theologian was employed in exegesis and polemics against the Arians; after that date it was devoted almost entirely to refuting the Nestorian heresy. The teaching of Nestorius was condemned in 431 by the Council of Ephesus at which Cyril presided, and Mary's title, Mother of God, was solemnly recognized. The incarnation is central to Cyril's theology. Only if Christ is consubstantial with the Father and with us can he save us, for the meeting ground between God and ourselves is the flesh of Christ. Through our kinship with Christ, the Word made flesh, we become children of God, and share in the filial relation of the Son with the Father.

# Twenty-Second Sunday
# in Ordinary Time

*Gospel:* Mark 7:1-8.14-15.21-23

You forget the commandment of God and cling to human traditions.

*Commentary:* Irenaeus

The Pharisees claimed that the traditions of their elders safeguarded the law, but in fact it contravened the law Moses had given. By saying: *Your merchants mix water with the wine* Isaiah shows that the elders mixed their watery tradition with God's strict commandment. In other words, they enjoined an adulterated law which went against the law, as the Lord also made clear when he asked them: *Why do you transgress God's commandment for the sake of your tradition?*

By their transgression they not only falsified God's law, mixing water with the wine, but they also set against it their own law, called to this day the Pharisaic law. In this their rabbis suppress some of the commandments, add new ones, and give others their own interpretation, thus making the law serve their own purposes.

Their desire to justify these traditions kept them from submitting to God's law that taught them about the coming of Christ. Instead, they even found fault with the Lord for healing on the sabbath, which was not forbidden by the law, for in a sense the law itself healed by causing circumcision to be performed on the sabbath. On the other hand, they found no fault with themselves for breaking God's commandment by their tradition and the Pharisaic law just mentioned, or for lacking the essence of the law, which is love for God.

That this is the first and greatest commandment, the second being love of our neighbor, the Lord taught by saying that the whole of the law and the prophets depend on these two commandments. He himself brought no greater commandment than this, but he renewed this same commandment by bidding his disciples love God with their whole heart, and their neighbor as themselves.

Paul also says that *love is the fulfillment of the law.* When all other charisms fail, faith, hope, and love remain, but the greatest of all is love. Knowledge is of no avail without the love of God, nor is understanding of mysteries, faith, or prophecy. Without love all are vain and profitless. Love on the other hand perfects a person, and one who loves God is perfect both in this world and the next, for we shall never stop loving God—the longer we gaze upon him the more our love for him will grow.

*(Against Heresies IV, 12, 1-2: SC 100, 508-14)*

---

**Irenaeus** (c. 140-200), who was born in Asia Minor and was in his youth a disciple of Saint Polycarp, became bishop of Lyons. Irenaeus wrote his principal work, *Against the Heresies,* to combat Gnostic dualism. At the heart of his theology is a vision of the unity, the recapitulation of all things in Christ. Just as all have sinned in one man, Adam, so all are offered salvation in Christ, the second Adam.

# Twenty-Third Sunday in Ordinary Time

*Gospel:* Mark 7:31-37

He has made the deaf hear and the dumb speak.

*Commentary:* Lawrence of Brindisi

Just as the divine law says that when God created the world *he saw all that he had made and it was very good,* so the gospel, speaking of our redemption and re-creation, affirms: *He has done all things well. A good tree bears good fruit; no good tree can bear bad fruit.* As fire can give out nothing but heat and is incapable of giving out cold; and as the sun gives out nothing but light and is incapable of giving out darkness, so God is incapable of doing anything but good, for he is infinite goodness and light. He is a sun giving out endless light, a fire producing endless warmth. *He has done all things well.*

And so today we must wholeheartedly unite with that holy throng in saying: *He has done all things well. He has made the deaf hear and the dumb speak.* Like Balaam's ass, this crowd certainly spoke under the inspiration of the Holy Spirit. Clearly it was the Holy Spirit who said through its mouth: *He has done all things well;* in other words he is truly God, because making the deaf hear and the dumb speak are things that only God can do. There is a transition here from the particular to the general. This man has worked a miracle that only God could work; therefore he is God, who has done all things well.

*He has done all things well.* The law says that all God did was good; the gospel says he has done all things well. Doing a good deed is not quite the same as doing it well. Many do good deeds but fail to do them well. The deeds of hypocrites, for example, are good, but they are done in the wrong spirit, with a perverse and defective intention. Everything God does, however, is not only good but is also done well. *The Lord is just in all his ways and holy in all his deeds. With wisdom you have done them all:* that is to say, most wisely and well. So *he has done all things well,* they say.

Now if God has done all his good works and done them well for our sake, knowing that we take pleasure in goodness, why I ask do we not endeavor to make all our works good and to do them well, knowing that such works are pleasing to God?

If you ask what we should do in order to enjoy the divine blessings for ever, I will tell you in a word. Since the Church is called the bride of Christ and of God, we must do what a good wife does for her husband. Then God will treat us as a good husband treats a dearly loved wife. This is what the Lord says through Hosea: *I will betroth you to myself with justice and integrity, with tenderness and compassion; I will betroth you to myself with faithfulness, and you shall know that I am the Lord.* So even in this present life we shall be happy, this world will be an earthly paradise for us; with the Hebrews we shall feast on heavenly manna in the desert of this life, if only we follow Christ's example by striving to do everything well, so that *he has done all things well* may be said of each one of us.

*(Eleventh Sunday after Pentecost I, 1.9.11.12:*
*Opera omnia, 8, 124.134.136-38).*

---

**Lawrence of Brindisi** (1559-1619) was born at Brindisi and educated at Venice. In 1575 he entered with the Capuchins and was sent to Padua to study philosophy and theology. He had a prodigious memory and was said to know the Scriptures by heart in the original. This enabled him to convert many Jews. Raised to a high degree of contemplation himself, he evangelized much of Europe, speaking to the hearts of those who heard him. From 1602 he served a term as minister general of the Capuchins. As chaplain to the imperial troops he led them into battle and to victory against the Turks on two occasions, armed only with a crucifix. He died at Lisbon while on an embassy. His writings include eight volumes of sermons, commentaries on Genesis and Ezekiel, and other didactic or controversial works. Pope John XXIII added his name to the list of doctors of the Church.

# Twenty-Fourth Sunday
# in Ordinary Time

*Gospel:* Mark 8:27-35

You are the Christ.

*Commentary:* Caesarius of Arles

When the Lord tells us in the gospel that anyone who wants to be his follower must renounce himself, the injunction seems harsh; we think he is imposing a burden on us. But an order is no burden when it is given by one who helps in carrying it out.

To what place are we to follow Christ if not where he has already gone? We know that he has risen and ascended into heaven: there, then, we must follow him. There is no cause for despair—by ourselves we can do nothing, but we have Christ's promise. Heaven was beyond our reach before our Head ascended there, but now, if we are his members, why should we despair of arriving there ourselves? Is there any reason? True, many fears and afflictions confront us in this world; but if we follow Christ, we shall reach a place of perfect happiness, perfect peace, and everlasting freedom from fear.

Yet let me warn anyone bent on following Christ to listen to Saint Paul: *One who claims to abide in Christ ought to walk as he walked.* Would you follow Christ? Then be humble as he was humble; do not scorn his lowliness if you want to reach his exaltation. Human sin made the road rough but Christ's resurrection leveled it; by passing over it himself he transformed the narrowest of tracks into a royal highway.

Two feet are needed to run along this highway; they are humility and charity. Everyone wants to get to the top—well, the first step to take is humility. Why take strides that are too big for you—do you want to fall instead of going up? Begin with the first step, humility, and you will already be climbing.

As well as telling us to renounce ourselves, our Lord and Savior said that we must take up our cross and follow him. What does it mean to take up one's cross? Bearing every annoyance patiently. That is following Christ. When someone begins to follow his way of life and his commandments, that person will meet resistance on every side. He or she will be opposed, mocked, even persecuted, and this not only by unbelievers but also by people who to all appearances belong to the body of Christ, though they are really excluded from it by their wickedness; people who, being Christians only in name, never stop persecuting true Christians.

If you want to follow Christ, then, take up his cross without delay. Endure injuries, do not be overcome by them. If we would fulfill the Lord's command: *If anyone wants to be my disciple, let him take up his cross and follow me,* we must strive with God's help to do as the Apostle says: *As long as we have food and clothing, let this content us.* Otherwise, if we seek more material goods than we need and desire to become rich, we may fall prey to temptation. The devil may trick us into wanting the many useless and harmful things that plunge people into ruin and destruction. May we be free from this temptation through the protection of our Lord, who lives and reigns with the Father and the Holy Spirit for ever and ever. Amen.

*(Sermon 159, 1.4-6: CCL 104, 650.652-54)*

---

**Caesarius of Arles** (c. 470-543) was born in Chalon on the Saône. In 489 he entered as a monk at Lérins. He was so outstanding in the perfection of his life and in his sense of justice that he was eventually made archbishop of Arles. He legislated for both nuns and monks, his *Rule for Virgins* being written for his sister Saint Caesaria, superior of a community of nuns. Influenced by Saint Augustine's teaching on grace, he successfully combatted semi-Pelagianism at the Council of Orange in 529. He was a celebrated preacher; his practical charity was such that he melted down church plate to relieve prisoners, and the quality of his prayer is reflected in his challenging statement: "One worships that on which one's mind is intent during prayer."

# Twenty-Fifth Sunday in Ordinary Time

*Gospel:* Mark 9:30-37

If anyone wishes to be first, let him make himself last of all and the servant of all.

*Commentary:* Theophylact

*As he was teaching his disciples the Lord said to them: "The Son of man will be delivered into the hands of men, and they will put him to death, but after his death, on the third day, he will rise again."*

The Lord always alternated prophecies of his passion with the performance of miracles, so that he should not be thought to have suffered through lack of power. Therefore, after imparting the grievous news that men would kill him, he added the joyful tidings that on the third day he would rise again. This was to teach us that joy always follows sorrow, and that we should not be uselessly distressed by painful events, but should rather have hope that better times will come.

*He came to Capernaum, and after entering the house he questioned the disciples: "What were you arguing about on the way?"* Now the disciples still saw things from a very human point of view, and they had been quarrelling amongst themselves about which of them was the greatest and the most esteemed by Christ. Yet the Lord did not restrain their desire for preeminent honor; indeed he wishes us to aspire to the most exalted rank. He does not however wish us to seize the first place, but rather to win the highest honor by humility.

He stood a child among them because he wants us to become childlike. A child has no desire for honor; it is not jealous, and it does not remember injuries. And he said: "If you become like that, you will receive a great reward, and if, moreover, for my sake, you honor others who are like that, you will receive the kingdom of heaven; for you will be receiving me, and in receiving me you receive the one who sent me."

You see then what great things humility, together with simplicity and guilelessness, can accomplish. It causes both the Son and the Father to dwell in us, and with them of course comes the Holy Spirit also.

*(Commentary on Mark's Gospel: PG 123, 588-89)*

---

**Theophylact** (c. 1050-1109), theologian and language scholar, studied at Constantinople. He taught rhetoric and was tutor to the imperial heir presumptive: hence his treatise on the *Education of Monarchs*. In 1078 he became archbishop of Ochrida in Bulgarian territory. While diffusing Byzantine culture among the Slavs, he allowed the use of Slavonic texts. He wrote commentaries on several books of the Old Testament and all of the New except Revelation. He especially stressed practical morality, as did Chrysostom, his model.

# Twenty-Sixth Sunday in Ordinary Time

*Gospel:* Mark 9:38-43.45.47-48

Anyone who is not against us is for us.

*Commentary:* Symeon the New Theologian

Do you not tremble when you hear God saying to you day after day throughout the whole of divine Scripture: *Let no evil word come from your mouth. Indeed I tell you that you will have to answer for a single careless word,* and: *You will receive a reward for a cup of cold water?*

My brothers, do not deceive yourselves. God loves us, and he is merciful and compassionate. I myself testify and acknowledge that it is his compassion that makes me confident of being saved. Nevertheless you must understand that this will be of no avail to those who refuse to repent and to keep God's commandments in every detail and with great fear. On the contrary, God will punish them more severely than people who are unbelievers and unbaptized.

O brothers, do not deceive yourselves; let there be no sin that seems small in your eyes, and that you treat lightly, as though it did no great harm to our souls. Right-minded servants make no distinction between a small sin and a great; if they offend by so much as a glance, a thought, or a word, they feel as if they have fallen away from the love of God, and I believe this is true. In fact, whoever has the slightest thought contrary to the divine will, and does not immediately repent and repel the assault of such a thought, but welcomes it and consents to it—that person is counted guilty of sin, and this is so even if he is unaware that his thought is sinful.

Consequently we need to be extremely vigilant and zealous, and to give much time to searching the divine Scriptures. The Savior's command, "Search the Scriptures" shows how profitable they are for us. So search them, and hold fast to what they say with great exactitude and faith. Then, when the divine Scriptures have given you an accurate knowledge of God's will, you will be able to distinguish without error between good and evil, and will not listen to every spirit, or be carried away by harmful thoughts.

You may be certain, my brothers, that nothing is so conducive to our salvation as following the divine commandments of the Savior. Nevertheless we shall have to shed many tears, and shall need great fear, great patience, and constant prayer before the import of even a word of the Master can be revealed to us. Only then shall we perceive the great mystery hidden in short sayings, and be ready to die for the smallest detail of the commandments of God. For the word of God is like a two-edged sword, cutting off and separating the soul from all bodily desire and sensation. More than that, it is like a blazing fire, because it stirs up zeal in our souls, and makes us disregard all the sorrows of life, consider every trial we encounter a joy, and desire and embrace death, so fearful to others, as life and the means of attaining life.

*(Catechesis I, 3: SC 96, 299-305)*

**Symeon the New Theologian** (949-1022) was born in Galata in Paphlagonia, and educated in Constantinople, where in 977 he entered the famous monastery of Studios. Soon afterward he transferred to the nearby monastery of Saint Mamas, was ordained priest in 980, and about three years later became abbot. During his twenty-five years of office he instilled a new fervor into his community, but opposition to his teaching forced him to resign in 1005 and in 1009 he was exiled to Palonkiton on the other side of the Bosphorus. He turned the ruined oratory of Saint Marina into another monastery, and although he was soon pardoned, chose to remain there until his death rather than compromise his teaching.

# Twenty-Seventh Sunday in Ordinary Time

*Gospel:* Mark 10:2-16

What God has joined together, no one must divide.

*Commentary:* Jacob of Serugh

In his mysterious plans the Father had destined a bride for his only Son and presented her to him under the guise of prophetic images. Moses appeared and with deft hand sketched a picture of bridegroom and bride but immediately drew a veil over it. In his book he wrote that a man should leave father and mother so as to be joined to his wife, that the two might in very truth become one. The prophet Moses spoke of man and woman in this way in order to foretell Christ and his Church. With a prophet's penetrating gaze he contemplated Christ becoming one with the Church through the mystery of water. He saw Christ even from the Virgin's womb drawing the Church to himself, and the Church in the water of baptism drawing Christ to herself. Bridegroom and bride were thus wholly united in a mystical manner, which is why Moses wrote that the two should become one.

With veiled face Moses contemplated Christ and the Church: the one he called "man" and the other "woman" so as not to reveal the full splendor of the reality. After the marriage celebration came Paul. He saw the veil covering their splendor and lifted it, revealing Christ and his Church to the whole world, and showing that it was they whom Moses had described in his prophetic vision. In an outburst of inspired joy the apostle exclaimed: This is a great mystery! He revealed the meaning of the veiled picture the prophet had called man and woman, declaring: *I know that it is Christ and his Church,* who were two before but have now become one.

Wives are not united to their husbands as closely as the Church is to the Son of God. What husband but our Lord ever died for his wife, and what bride ever chose a crucified man as her husband? Who ever gave his blood as a gift to his wife except the one who died on the cross and sealed the marriage bond with his wounds? Who was ever seen lying dead at his own wedding banquet with his wife at his side seeking to console herself by embracing him? At what other celebration, at what other feast is the bridegroom's body distributed to the guests in the form of bread?

Death separates wives from their husbands, but in this case it is death that unites the bride to her beloved. He died on the cross, bequeathed his body to his glorious spouse, and now every day she receives and consumes it at his table. She consumes it under the form of bread, and under the form of the wine that she drinks, so that the whole world may know that they are no longer two but one.

*(Guéranger: The Liturgical Year 3, 1023-25)*

---

**Jacob of Serugh** (c. 451-521), a Syrian Orthodox poet, was educated at Edessa and ordained priest. He did much to encourage his people during their sufferings at the hands of the Persians. In 519 he was made bishop of Batnae near Edessa. His metrical homilies won him the title "Flute of the Holy Spirit." His writings include also letters, sermons, biographies, and hymns.

# Twenty-Eighth Sunday in Ordinary Time

*Gospel:* Mark 10:17-30

Go and sell everything you own and follow me.

*Commentary:* John Henry Newman

All through our life Christ is calling us. He called us first in baptism, but afterwards also; whether we obey his voice or not, he graciously calls us still. If we fall from our baptism, he calls us to repent; if we are striving to fulfil our calling, he calls us on from grace to grace, and from holiness to holiness, while life is given us. Abraham was called from his home, Peter from his nets, Matthew from his office, Elisha from his farm, Nathanael from his retreat; we are all in course of calling, on and on, from one thing to another, having no resting place, but mounting towards our eternal rest, and obeying one command only to have another put upon us. He calls us again and again, in order to justify us again and again—and again and again, and more and more, to sanctify and glorify us.

It were well if we understood this; but we are slow to master the great truth, that Christ is, as it were, walking among us, and by his hand, or eye, or voice, bidding us follow him. We do not understand that his call is a thing which takes place now. We think it took place in the Apostles' day; but we do not believe in it, we do not look out for it in our own case. We have not eyes to see the Lord; far different from the beloved Apostle, who knew Christ even when the rest of the disciples knew him not. When he stood on the shore after his resurrection, and bade them cast the net into the sea, *that disciple whom Jesus loved said to Peter, It is the Lord.*

Now what I mean is this: that they who are living religiously, have from time to time truths they did not know before, or had no need to consider, brought before them forcibly; truths which involve duties, which are in fact precepts, and claim obedience. In this and such-like ways Christ calls us now. There is nothing miraculous or extraordinary in his dealings with us. He works through our natural faculties and circumstances of life. Still what happens to us in providence is in all essential respects what his voice was to those whom he addressed when on earth: whether he commands by a visible presence, or by a voice, or by our consciences, it matters not, so that we feel it to be a command. If it is a command, it may be obeyed or disobeyed; it may be accepted as Samuel or St. Paul accepted it, or put aside after the manner of the young man who had great possessions.

We need not fear spiritual pride in following Christ's call, if we follow it as people in earnest. Earnestness has no time to compare itself with the state of others; earnestness is simply set on doing God's will. It simply says, *Speak, Lord, for thy servant heareth; Lord, what wilt thou have me to do?* Oh that we had more of this spirit! Oh that we could take that simple view of things, as to feel that the one thing which lies before us is to please God!

Let us beg and pray Him day by day to reveal Himself to our souls more fully; to quicken our senses; to give us sight and hearing, taste and touch of the world to come; so to work within us that we may sincerely say, *Thou shalt guide me with Thy counsel, and after that receive me to glory. Whom have I in heaven but Thee? and there is none upon earth that I desire in comparison of Thee: my flesh and my heart faileth; but God is the strength of my heart, and my portion for ever.*

(*Parochial and Plain Sermons 8, 23-25.31-32*)

---

**Newman, John Henry** (1801-90) was born in London and brought up in the Church of England. He went up to Trinity College, Oxford in 1817, became a Fellow of Oriel five years later, was ordained deacon in 1824 and appointed Vicar of Saint Mary's, Oxford, in 1832. The impact of his sermons was tremendous. He was the leading spirit in the Tractarian Movement (1833-41) and the condemnation of Tract 90 led to his resignation from Saint Mary's in 1843. Two years later he was received into the Catholic Church. He was ordained in Rome and founded a house of Oratorians in Birmingham. Newman's *Essay on the Development Christian Doctrine* throws light on his withdrawal of previous objections to Roman Catholicism; his *Apologia* reveals the deepest motives underlying his outward attitudes, and the *Grammar of Assent* clarifies the subjective content of commitment to faith. In 1879 he was made a cardinal and he died at Edgbaston in 1890.

# Twenty-Ninth Sunday in Ordinary Time

*Gospel:* Mark 10:35-45

The Son of man came to give his life as a ransom for many.

*Commentary:* John Chrysostom

When the ten disciples were indignant with James and John for separating themselves from their company in the hope of obtaining the highest honor, Jesus corrected the disorderly passions of both groups. Notice how he did it.

*He called them to him and said: Gentile rulers lord it over their people, and holders of high office make their authority felt. This must not happen among you. On the contrary, whoever wants to be first among you must be last of all.*

You see that what the two brothers wanted was to be first, greatest, and highest: rulers, one might almost say, of the others. So, revealing their secret thoughts, Jesus put a curb on this ambition, saying: *Whoever wants to be first among you must become the servant of all.* If you wish to take precedence and to have the highest honors, aim for whatever is lowest and worst: to be the most insignificant and humble of all, of less account than anyone else; to put yourselves after the others. It is virtue of this kind that wins the honor you aspire to, and you have an outstanding example of it near at hand. *For the Son of man came not to be served but to serve, and to give his life as a ransom for many.* This is what will make you illustrious and far-famed. See what is happening in my case. I do not seek glory and honor, yet by acting in this way I am gaining innumerable blessings.

The fact is that before the incarnation and self-abasement of Christ the whole world was in a state of ruin and decay, but when he humbled himself he lifted the world up. He annuled the curse, put an end to death, opened paradise, destroyed sin, flung wide the gates of heaven, and introduced there the firstfruits of our race. He filled the world with faith in God, drove out error, restored truth, caused our firstfruits to ascend a royal throne, and gained innumerable blessings beyond the power of myself or anyone else to describe in words. Before he humbled himself he was known only to the angels, but after his self-abasement he was recognized by the whole human race.

*(Homilies Against the Anomeans, VIII: Bareille 2, 253-54)*

---

**John Chrysostom** (c. 347-407) was born at Antioch and studied under Diodore of Tarsus, the leader of the Antiochene school of theology. After a period of great austerity as a hermit, he returned to Antioch where he was ordained deacon in 381 and priest in 386. From 386 to 397 it was his duty to preach in the principal church of the city, and his best homilies, which earned him the title "Chrysostomos" or "the golden-mouthed," were preached at this time. In 397 Chrysostom became patriarch of Constantinople, where his efforts to reform the court, clergy, and people led to his exile in 404 and finally to his death from the hardships imposed on him. Chrysostom stressed the divinity of Christ against the Arians and his full humanity against the Apollinarians, but he had no speculative bent. He was above all a pastor of souls, and was one of the most attractive personalities of the early Church.

127

# Thirtieth Sunday
# in Ordinary Time

*Gospel:* Mark 10:46-52

Master, grant that I may see.

*Commentary:* Clement of Alexandria

*The commandment of the Lord shines clearly, enlightening the eyes.* Receive Christ, receive power to see, receive your light, "that you may plainly recognize both God and man." *More delightful than gold and precious stones, more desirable than honey and the honeycomb* is the Word that has enlightened us. How could he not be desirable, he who illumined minds buried in darkness, and endowed with clear vision "the light-bearing eyes" of the soul?

"Despite the other stars, without the sun the whole world would be plunged in darkness." So likewise we ourselves, had we not known the Word and been enlightened by him, should have been no better off than plump poultry fattened in the dark, simply reared for death. Let us open ourselves to the light, then, and so to God. Let us open ourselves to the light, and become disciples of the Lord. For he promised his Father: *I will make known your name to my brothers and sisters, and praise you where they are assembled.*

Sing his praises, then, Lord, and make known to me your Father, who is God. Your words will save me, your song instruct me. Hitherto I have gone astray in my search for God; but now that you light my path, Lord, and I find God through you, and receive the Father from you, I become co-heir with you, since you were not ashamed to own me as your brother.

Let us, then, shake off forgetfulness of truth, shake off the mist of ignorance and darkness that dims our eyes, and contemplate the true God, after first raising this song of praise to him: "All hail, O Light!" For upon us buried in darkness, imprisoned in the shadow of death, a heavenly light has shone, a light of a clarity surpassing the sun's, and of a sweetness exceeding any this earthly life can offer. That light is eternal life, and those who receive it live. Night, on the other hand, is afraid of the light, and melting away in terror gives place to the day of the Lord. Unfailing light has penetrated everywhere, and sunset has turned into dawn. This is the meaning of the new creation; for the Sun of Righteousness, pursuing his course through the universe, visits all alike, in imitation of his Father, *who makes his sun rise upon all,* and bedews everyone with his truth.

He it is who has changed sunset into dawn and death into life by his crucifixion; he it is who has snatched the human race from perdition and exalted it to the skies. Transplanting what was corruptible to make it incorruptible, transforming earth into heaven, he, God's gardener, points the way to prosperity, prompts his people to good works, "reminds them how to live" according to the truth, and bestows on us the truly great and divine heritage of the Father, which cannot be taken away from us. He deifies us by his heavenly teaching, instilling his laws into our minds, and writing them on our hearts. What are the laws he prescribes? That all, be they of high estate or low, shall know God. *And I will be merciful to them,* God says, *and I will remember their sin no more.*

Let us accept the laws of life, let us obey God's promptings. Let us learn to know him, so that he may be merciful to us. Although he stands in no need of it, let us pay God our debt of gratitude in willing obedience as a rent, so to speak, which we owe him for our lodging here below.

*(Exhortation to the Greeks 11: SC 2, 181-83)*

---

**Clement of Alexandria** (c. 150-215) was born at Athens of pagan parents. Nothing is known of his early life nor of the reasons for his conversion. He was the pupil and the assistant of Pantaenus, the director of the catechetical school of Alexandria, whom he succeeded about the year 200. In 202 Clement left Alexandria because of the persecution of Septimus Severus, and resided in Cappadocia with his pupil, Alexander, later bishop of Jerusalem. Clement may be considered the founder of speculative theology. He strove to protect and deepen faith by the use of Greek philosophy. Central in his teaching is his doctrine of the Logos, who as divine reason is the teacher of the world and its lawgiver. Clement's chief work is the trilogy, *Exhortation to the Greeks, The Teacher,* and *Miscellanies.*

# Thirty-First Sunday in Ordinary Time

*Gospel:* Mark 12:28-34

This is the first commandment, and the second is similar to it.

*Commentary:* Francis de Sales

Because God created us in his own image and likeness, he ordained that our love for one another should be in the image and likeness of the love we owe him, our God. He said: *You must love the Lord your God with your whole heart. This is the first and greatest commandment. The second is like it: You must love your neighbor as yourself.*

What is our reason for loving God? God himself is the reason we love him; we love him because he is the supreme and infinite goodness. What is our reason for loving ourselves? Surely because we are the image and likeness of God. And since all men and women possess this same dignity we love them as ourselves, that is, as holy and living images of the Godhead. It is as such that we belong to God through a kinship so close and a dependence so lovable that he does not hesitate to call himself our Father, and to name us his children. It is as such that we are capable of being united to him in the fruition of his sovereign goodness and joy. It is as such that we receive his grace and that our spirits are associated with his most Holy Spirit and rendered, in a sense, *sharers in the divine nature.*

So it is then that the same charity produces together acts of the love of God and of our neighbor. As Jacob saw that the same ladder touching heaven and earth was used by the angels both for ascending and descending, so we can be sure that the same charity cherishes both God and our neighbor, raising us even to spiritual union with God, and bringing us back to loving companionship with our neighbors. It must always be understood, however, that we love our neighbors for this reason, that they are made in the image and likeness of God, created to communicate in his goodness, share in his grace, and rejoice in his glory.

To have a Christian love for our neighbors is to love God in them, or them in God; it is to cherish God alone for his own sake, and his creatures for love of him. When we look upon our neighbors, created in the image and likeness of God, should we not say to each other: "Look at these people he has made—are they not like their maker?" Should we not be drawn irresistibly toward them, embrace them, and be moved to tears for love of them? Should we not call down upon them a hundred blessings? And why? For love of them? No indeed, since we cannot be sure whether, of themselves, they are worthy of love or hate. Then why? For love of God, who created them in his own image and likeness, and so capable of sharing in his goodness, grace, and glory; for love of God, I say, unto whom they exist, from whom they exist, through whom they exist, in whom they exist, for whom they exist, and whom they resemble in a very special manner.

This is why divine Love not only repeatedly commands us to love our neighbors, but also itself produces this love and pours it out into our hearts, since they bear its own image and likeness; for just as we are the image of God, so our holy love for one another is the true image of our heavenly love for God.

*(Guérin, Treatise on the Love of God II, 10, 11, 193-95)*

---

**Francis de Sales** (1567-1622), born on the family estate of Sales in Savoy, was educated at Annecy, Paris, and Padua. In 1593 he was ordained priest and in the following year courageously set out to win back the people of the Chablais from Calvinism to Catholicism. Thanks to his ardent zeal and habitual gentleness he made eight thousand converts within two years. He was appointed coadjutor to the bishop of Geneva and in 1602 succeeded to the see. Together with Saint Jane Frances de Chantal he founded the Order of the Visitation. He died at Lyons when returning from Avignon. His best known writings are the *Introduction to a Devout Life* and the *Treatise on the Love of God*. In 1877 he was declared to be a doctor of the Church.

# Thirty-Second Sunday in Ordinary Time

*Gospel:* Mark 12:38-44

The poor widow has put more in than all who contributed.

*Commentary:* Paulinus of Nola

*What have you,* asks the Apostle, *that you have not received?* This means, beloved, that we should not be miserly, regarding possessions as our own, but should rather invest what has been entrusted to us. We have been entrusted with the administration and use of temporal wealth for the common good, not with the everlasting ownership of private property. If you accept the fact that ownership on earth is only for a time, you can earn eternal possessions in heaven.

Call to mind the widow who forgot herself in her concern for the poor, and, thinking only of the life to come, gave away all her means of subsistence, as the judge himself bears witness. Others, he says, have given of their superfluous wealth; but she, possessed of only two small coins and more needy perhaps than many of the poor—though in spiritual riches she surpassed all the wealthy—she thought only of the world to come, and had such a longing for heavenly treasure that she gave away, all at once, whatever she had that was derived from the earth and destined to return there.

Let us then invest with the Lord what he has given us, for we have nothing that does not come from him: we are dependent upon him for our very existence. And we ourselves particularly, who have a special and a greater debt, since God not only created us but purchased us as well—what can we regard as our own when we do not possess even ourselves?

But let us rejoice that we have been bought at a great price, the price of the Lord's own blood, and that because of this we are no longer worthless slaves. For there is a freedom that is baser than slavery, namely, freedom from justice. Whoever has that kind of freedom is a slave of sin and a prisoner of death. So let us give back to the Lord the gifts he has given us; let us give to him who receives in the person of every poor man or woman. Let us give gladly, I say, and great joy will be ours when we receive his promised reward.

*(Letter 34, 2-4: CSEL 29, 305-06)*

---

**Paulinus of Nola** (353/54-431), was the son of a noble family of Bordeaux. He seems to have received a good education, and sat at the feet of the famous Ausonius. After a brief public career he was baptized, and in agreement with his wife Therasia retired from the world, after dividing his fortune between the Church and the poor. He was ordanied priest at Barcelona in 394. Shortly afterward he settled at Nola, near the tomb of Saint Felix, and with his wife opened a home for monks and the poor. In 409 he was ordained bishop. Paulinus was the foremost Christian Latin poet of this period, and the friend of Martin of Tours, Ambrose, and Augustine. Many of his letters survive. They are filled with Christian hope and charity and reflect the Church's understanding of the mystery of salvation.

# Thirty-Third Sunday in Ordinary Time

*Gospel:* Mark 13:24-32

He shall gather his elect from the four winds.

*Commentary:* Gregory Palamas

All those who hold to true faith in our Lord Jesus Christ and show proof of their faith by good works, guarding themselves from sins or cleansing themselves from their stains by confession and repentance; who practice the virtues opposed to those sins—temperance, chastity, love, almsgiving, justice, and fair dealing—all these, I say, will rise again to hear the king of heaven himself saying to them: *Come, my Father's blessed ones, inherit the kingdom prepared for you since the creation of the world.* So will they reign with Christ, receiving as their inheritance that heavenly kingdom which cannot be shaken, living for ever in the ineffable light that knows no evening and is interrupted by no night, having fellowship with all the saints who have lived from the beginning of time, and enjoying delights beyond description in Abraham's embrace, where all pain has fled away, and all grief and groaning.

For just as there is a harvest for inanimate sheaves of wheat, so for the rational wheat which is the human race, there is a harvest that cuts people away from unbelief, and gathers into faith those who accept the proclamation of the good news. The reapers of this harvest are the Lord's apostles and their successors, and in the course of time the teachers of the Church. Of them the Lord said: *The reaper receives his wages, and gathers a crop for eternal life,* for teachers who instruct others in piety will in their turn receive from God such recompense as befits those who gather the obedient into eternal life.

But there is yet another harvest: the transfer of each one of us by death from this present life into that which is to come. The reapers of this harvest are not the apostles but the angels, who have a greater responsibility than the apostles, because after the harvesting they sort out the good and separate them from the wicked like wheat from darnel. The good they send on to the kingdom of heaven, but the wicked they throw into hell fire.

As for us, who in this present age are God's chosen people, a priestly race, the Church of the living God separated from all the impious and ungodly, may we be found separated from the darnel in the age to come as well, and united to those who are saved in Christ our Lord, who is blessed for ever. Amen.

*(Homily 26: PG 151, 340-41)*

---

**Gregory Palamas** (1296-1359) was born at Constantinople, and prepared by the piety of his parents for a monastic vocation. At the age of about twenty he became a monk of Mount Athos. In 1347 he was made bishop of Thessalonica. Gregory stressed the biblical teaching that the human body and soul form a single united whole. On this basis he defended the physical exercises used by the Hesychasts in prayer, although he saw these only as a means to an end for those who found them helpful. He followed Saint Basil the Great and Saint Gregory of Nyssa in teaching that although no created intelligence can ever comprehend God in his essence, he can be directly experienced through his uncreated "energies," through which he manifests himself to and is present in the world. God's substance and his energies are distinct from one another, but they are also inseparable. One of these energies is the uncreated divine light, which was seen by the apostles on Mount Tabor. At times this is an inward illumination; at other times it is outwardly manifested.

# Thirty-Fourth Sunday
# in Ordinary Time

*Gospel:* John 18:33-37

You say that I am king.

*Commentary:* Augustine

L isten, everyone, Jews and Gentiles, circumcised and uncircumcised. Listen, all kings of the earth. I am no hindrance to your rule in this world, for *my kingdom is not of this world.* Banish the groundless fear that filled Herod the Great on hearing that Christ was born. More cruel in his fear than in his anger, he put many children to death, so that Christ also would die. But *my kingdom is not of this world,* says Christ. What further reassurance do you seek? Come to the kingdom not of this world. Be not enraged by fear, but come by faith. In a prophecy Christ also said: *He,* that is, God the Father, *has made me king on Zion his holy mountain.* But that Zion and that mountain are not of this world.

What in fact is Christ's kingdom? It is simply those who believe in him, those to whom he said: *You are not of this world, even as I am not of this world.* He willed, nevertheless, that they should be in the world, which is why he prayed to the Father: *I ask you not to take them out of the world, but to protect them from the evil one.* So here also he did not say: *My kingdom is not* in this world, but *is not of this world.* And when he went on to prove this by declaring: *If my kingdom were of this world, my servants would have fought to save me from being handed over to the Jews,* he concluded by saying not "my kingdom is not here," but *my kingdom is not from here.*

Indeed, his kingdom is here until the end of time, and until the harvest it will contain weeds. The harvest is the end of the world, when the reapers, who are the angels, will come *and gather out of his kingdom all causes of sin;* and this could not happen if his kingdom were not here. But even so, it is not from here, for it is in exile in the world. Christ says to his kingdom: *You are not of the world, but I have chosen you out of the world.* They were indeed of the world when they belonged to the prince of this world, before they became his kingdom. Though created by the true God, everyone born of the corrupt and accursed stock of Adam is of the world. On the other hand, everyone who is reborn in Christ becomes the kingdom which is no longer of the world. For so has God snatched us from the powers of darkness, and brought us into the kingdom of his beloved Son: that kingdom of which he said: *My kingdom is not of this world; my kingly power does not come from here.*

*(Homilies on the Gospel of John 115, 2: CCL 36, 644-45)*

**Augustine** (354-430) was born at Thagaste in Africa and received a Christian education, although he was not baptized until 387. In 391 he was ordained priest and in 395 he became coadjutor bishop to Valerius of Hippo, whom he succeeded in 396. Augustine's theology was formulated in the course of his struggle with three heresies: Manichaeism, Donatism, and Pelagianism. His writings are voluminous and his influence on subsequent theology immense. He molded the thought of the Middle Ages down to the thirteenth century. Yet he was above all a pastor and a great spiritual writer.

# *Presentation of the Lord*

*Gospel:* Luke 2:22-40 or 22-32

My eyes have seen your saving power.

*Commentary:* Timothy of Jerusalem

*The just live for ever and their reward is in the Lord and their hope in the Most High.* Time will not suffice for us to recount the virtues of all the saints, so let us consider for the moment the last of the righteous men of old. Whom do I mean? Simeon, whose name is given in the gospel according to Luke. He stands both first and last, being the last to live under the law and the first to live by grace. In observance he was a Jew, in thanksgiving a Christian; by training he was a lawyer, but by knowledge of God an ambassador.

This Simeon, whose story has just been read to us, was plucked from the ill-fame of the Pharisees like a rose from thorns, and became the first to win renown through the gift of grace. Because of his righteousness God revealed to him, while he was still in the body, that he would not depart this present transitory life until his own arms had enfolded life eternal, our Lord Jesus Christ. Simeon the righteous, who before the incarnation had longed to see the Lord, saw him incarnate, recognized him and took him in his arms. Then he cried for release from the prison of his body, calling as a servant on the Lord of all who appeared as a child, in the words you have just heard: *Now, Lord, you let your servant go in peace as you promised, for my eyes have seen your salvation.*

I have seen, allow me to leave, do not keep me here. Let me depart in peace, do not keep me in distress. I have seen, let me go: I have seen your glory, seen the angels dancing, the archangels praising you, creation leaping for joy, a way made between heaven and earth. Now let me depart, do not keep me here below.

Do not let me see the insolence of fellow Jews, the crown of thorns being plaited, a slave beating you, or a spear being thrust into you: do not let me see the sun darkened, the moon fading, the elements altered: do not let me see you broken on a cross, the rocks split asunder, the veil of the temple rent. The elements themselves will not endure this audacity, and will share in the suffering of the Lord. *Now, Lord, you let your servant go in peace as you promised, for my eyes have seen your salvation, which you have prepared in the sight of all the nations.*

*(Sermon on Simeon: PG 86/1, 239-42)*

---

**Timothy of Jerusalem**, who lived between the sixth and eighth centuries, is known only from five sermons on biblical subjects, of which only that on the presentation of Christ in the temple is preserved under his own name. His homily on the cross and transfiguration of the Lord is said to be by one Timothy of Antioch, while the other three are attributed to Saint Athanasius. Timothy was the first to express the opinion that the Virgin Mary did not die.

# Birth of Saint John the Baptist

*Gospel:* Luke 1:57-60.80

John is his name.

*Commentary:* Maximus of Turin

Our feelings of piety and devotion bid us rejoice today in the birth of Saint John the Baptist. He was chosen by God to come and proclaim him who is the joy of the human race and the bliss of heaven. He is the new witness from whose lips the world heard that our Redeemer, the Lamb of God, was at hand. He, the trustworthy messenger of so great a mystery, was the witness whose birth was announced by an angel to parents who had given up hope of offspring. What person of good sense, discerning the hand of heaven in his birth, would not believe that he proclaimed divine mysteries? For he was not yet a child and was being carried partly formed in the womb when, by the privilege of the grace bestowed on him, he filled the heart of his blessed mother with eternal joy, and before his birth she made known the fruitfulness of her once barren womb. Elizabeth said to Mary: *Why, as the sound of your greeting reached my ears, the child in my womb leapt for joy! How is it that I am honored by a visit from the mother of my Lord?* It is not surprising that this elderly woman was endowed with the gift of foreknowledge, since she was to give birth to the herald of the most high God.

Elizabeth's barrenness became her glory, for because her fruitfulness was delayed she obtained by the gift of a single child the honor of all posterity. While in their old age she and her husband were lamenting her unfruitfulness, she unexpectedly brought forth not merely a son for herself but the herald of eternal salvation for the whole world. Such a great herald was he that by anticipating the grace of his future ministry, he gave his mother the spirit of prophecy, and by the power of the name assigned to him by the angel, he opened the mouth of his father Zechariah, which had been sealed by doubt.

For Zechariah had lost the power of speech not permanently, but so that the miraculous restoration of his voice might give heavenly testimony to the prophetic child. The priest who used to speak to the people became dumb so that his public silence might bring the mystery of the sacred birth to the notice of the entire people, and they would not dare to disbelieve.

Of him whose birth his father doubted, incurring the punishment of being unable to speak, the Evangelist says: *He himself was not the light, but came to give testimony to the light so that everyone might believe through him.* Indeed he was not the light, but because he was worthy to give testimony to the true light, he was wholly in the light. Therefore let us all give honor to the most blessed John by celebrating this day of his birth with great joy, for before anyone else he recognized the everlasting light of heaven which was going to dispel the darkness of the world, and he was the first to point it out.

*(Sermon 57: PL 57, 647-48)*

---

**Maximus of Turin** was bishop of Turin, but nothing else is known about his life except that he died in the reign of Honorius and Theodosius the Younger (408-23). From his surviving sermons it is clear that he must have been a zealous and effective pastor.

# Saints Peter and Paul

*Gospel:* Matthew 16:13-19

You are Peter, and I will give you the keys of the kingdom of heaven.

*Commentary:* Theophanes Cerameus

**B**ut who do you say that I am? It is as though the Lord said: "The general opinion is clearly much divided and uncertain, but since you have known me for such a long time, what is your judgment in the matter?" The rest of the disciples were lost for an answer; some perhaps were undecided, while others feared to seem rash. It was Peter, their leader, who became the spokesman for his companions. Transcending in thought the world of perception, he flew through the air to the heavens above, leaving the stars behind him and reaching further than the highest sphere. So he arrived in the spirit world, crossed the fiery rivers of the seraphim, and was taught by the Father about the nobility of his only-begotten Son. Then he uttered that theological pronouncement: *You are the Christ, the Son of the living God.*

What was the Savior's reply? *Blessed are you, Simon Bar Jonah, for flesh and blood has not revealed this to you.* In other words, "It was not by remaining in your body of flesh and blood that you received this revelation about me; you had to be entirely outside the world of the senses to be initiated into the divine mysteries." In the same way, when Paul said that he had been raised to the third heaven and had heard words too sacred to tell, he had no need of bodily awareness when contemplating spiritual truths. As he himself declared: *Whether in the body or out of the body I do not know.*

*And I tell you that you are Peter, and on this rock I will build my Church.* "Because you are Peter," our Lord said, "you will become the rock of faith, the foundation stone of the Church, and the principal means for its spiritual construction. On this confession of yours that I am both Son of God and Son of Man the Church's foundation stone will be laid; for such a foundation provides a secure basis on which to build the remaining doctrines."

*And the gates of hell shall not prevail against it.* The gates of hell which will not prevail against the Church are no doubt the tyrants who persecute it, and the founders of heresies. They are called the gates of hell figuratively because they drag their followers toward the snares of hell.

*And I will give you the keys of the kingdom of heaven.* The Lord did not say "I give you now," but "I will give you," foretelling what would happen after the resurrection. It was then that he granted Peter the grace of the Holy Spirit and the power of binding and loosing, and appointed him to be shepherd of his human flock. But what are the keys, and of what kind of door is Peter appointed the guardian? Christ is the door, as he himself declared; and the key to that door is faith, the faith which he entrusted to his chief disciple.

The Lord has given the keys to Peter and his successors, then, to keep the door to the kingdom of heaven inaccessible to heretics and impenetrable by them, but easy for the faithful to enter, thus confirming his declaration: *Without being born of water and the Spirit no one can enter the kingdom of heaven.* The opponents and enemies of the faith are called the gates of hell, but the Lord Emmanuel is called the door and gateway to the kingdom of heaven, and he eagerly calls out to everyone: *Whoever enters through me will be saved* and *Enter through the narrow gate and shun the wide streets that lead to hell.*

(Homily 55: PG 132, 960-65)

---

**Theophanes Cerameus** (12th century) came from the ancient Greek colonies of Sicily and Southern Italy. His surname, Cerameus, the Greek word for "potter," was common, and so caused some confusion in his identification. Formerly he was thought to have been archbishop of Taormina in Sicily, but more recent research has shown that he was in fact archbishop of Rossano, Southern Italy, from 1129 to 1152. His sermons, written in Greek, were outstanding for their time, being remarkable especially for their simplicity and oratorical skill.

# Transfiguration of the Lord

*Gospel:* Mark 9:2-10

This is my Son, my beloved.

*Commentary:* John of Damascus

A*bright cloud overshadowed them,* and seeing within it Jesus the Savior with Moses and Elijah, the disciples were filled with great fear.

Of old when Moses saw God he experienced the divine darkness, indicating the symbolic nature of the law; for as Paul has written, *the law contained only a shadow of the things to come, not the reality itself.* In the past Israel could not look at the transient glory on the face of Moses; but we, beholding the glory of the Lord with unveiled faces, are being transformed from one degree of glory to another by the Lord who is the Spirit. The cloud, therefore, that overshadowed the disciples was not one of threatening darkness but of light; for the mystery hidden from past ages has been revealed to show us perpetual and eternal glory. Moses and Elijah, representing the law and the prophets, stood by the Savior because he whom the law and the prophets proclaimed was present in Jesus, the giver of life.

And a voice from the cloud said: *This is my beloved Son.* He who is seen in human form, who became man only yesterday, who lives humbly in the midst of us, and whose face is now shining, is he who is. *This is my beloved Son,* the eternal, the only begotten of the only God, he who proceeds timelessly and eternally from me, his Father; who did not begin to exist after me, but is from me and with me and in me from all eternity.

It was by the Father's good pleasure that his only begotten Son and Word became incarnate; it was by the Father's good pleasure that the salvation of the world was achieved through his only begotten Son; it was the Father's good pleasure which brought about the union of the whole universe in his only begotten Son. For humanity is a microcosm linking in itself all visible and invisible being, sharing as it does in the nature of both, and so it must surely have pleased the Lord, the Creator and ruler of the universe, for divinity and humanity and thus all creation to be united in his only begotten and consubstantial Son, *so that God might be all in all.*

*This is my Son,* the radiance of my glory, who bears the stamp of my own nature, through whom I created the angels, through whom the vault of heaven was made firm and the earth established. He upholds the universe by his powerful word, and by the Spirit which proceeds from his mouth, that is the life-giving and guiding Spirit. *Listen to him.* Whoever receives him, receives me who sent him by the authority not of a stern master but of a father. As a man he is sent, but as God he abides in me and I in him. Whoever refuses to honor my only begotten Son refuses to honor me, his Father who sent him. *Listen to him,* for he has the words of eternal life.

*(Homily on the Transfiguration of the Lord 17-18:*
*PG 96, 572-73)*

---

**John of Damascus** (c. 576 - c. 649) left Damascus, where he had been a revenue official of the Caliph, about the turn of the century to enter the laura of Saint Sabas near Jerusalem. Known as the last of the Greek Fathers, whose *Fount of Wisdom* might be described as the *Summa* of the Orthodox, he was a compiler rather than an original thinker. Notable among his other writings are the three discourses against the iconoclasts and sermons on the liturgical mysteries and Our Lady. He is regarded as one of the greatest hymn writers of the Eastern Church.

# Assumption of the Blessed Virgin Mary

*Gospel:* Luke 1:39-56

The Mighty One has done great things to me and has exalted the humble.

*Commentary:* Attributed to Modestus of Jerusalem

When she had successfully completed her voyage through life, the human ship which had carried her God reached the haven of perfect peace beside the helmsman of the world who, with her help, had saved the human race from the flood of godlessness and sin, and given it life. He who gave one law on Sinai, and issued another from Zion, our God himself, sent there to have the ark which he had sanctified brought to him, the ark of which David her ancestor had sung: *Go up, Lord, to your resting place, you and the ark which you have sanctified.*

This ark was not drawn by oxen like the Mosaic ark of old, but guided and guarded by a heavenly army of holy angels. It was not an ark made by hands and plated with gold, but a living ark created by God, wholly luminous with the radiance of the all-holy and life-giving Spirit who had visited her. Within this ark there was no jar of manna, no tablets of the covenant, but instead the bestower of manna and of the promised blessings of eternity, the Lord of the new and old covenants, who from this ark came into the world as a child and freed those who believe in him from the curse of the law. This ark did not have Aaron's rod within and the glorious Cherubim above, but possessed the incomparably greater glory of being herself the rod of Jesse, and of being overshadowed by the divine, the almighty power of the supremely exalted Father. And instead of preceding the Hebrew people like the earlier ark, this ark followed God when he appeared on earth in the body received from her. Blessed by angels and humans alike to the glory of him who exalts her above all creatures in heaven and on earth, her holy lips exclaimed: *My soul proclaims the greatness of the Lord, my spirit rejoices in God my Savior.*

In order to shine out clearly, this light-bringing spiritual dawn came to dwell in the radiance of the Sun of Righteousness, in obedience to him who rose by his own power to give light to all creation. Through her the splendor that outshines even the rays of the sun sheds his light upon us in mercy and compassion, stirring up in the souls of believers the desire to imitate as far as they can his divine kindness and goodness. For Christ our God, who from this maiden who remained always a virgin and from the Holy Spirit had clothed himself in a human body possessed of soul and mind, called her to himself and clothed her in immortality, since she was his own flesh and blood. Because she was his most holy mother, he bestowed on her the highest honor by making her his heir; as the Psalmist sings: *The queen stands on your right robed in raiment wrought with gold and divers colors.*

Today the human tent which in a wonderful way received God, the Lord of heaven and earth, in the flesh is taken away. She, his own flesh and blood, is made by him immortal, to become together with him for ever strong to defend, protect, and save all of us who are Christians.

*(The Falling Asleep of the Virgin Mary 4-5: PG 86/2, 3288-89)*

# Triumph of the Cross

*Gospel:* John 3:13-17

The Son of Man must be lifted up.

*Commentary:* Bede

A s Moses lifted up the serpent in the wilderness, so must the Son *of man be lifted up, so that all who believe in him may not perish but may have eternal life.* With the wonderful skill he has in imparting heavenly teaching, the Lord of the teachers of the Mosaic law shows us that law's spiritual meaning, as he recalls the old history and explains its symbolic reference to his own passion and to our salvation.

The Book of Numbers relates that the Israelites, wearied by the long hard journey in the wilderness, grumbled against the Lord and Moses, and therefore the Lord sent fiery serpents among them. Many died of their bites, and when the people cried out to Moses and he prayed for them, the Lord commanded him to make a bronze serpent and set it up as a sign. *Those who are bitten,* he said, *have but to look at it and they will live;* and so it happened.

Now the bites of fiery serpents are the evil temptations to sin that bring spiritual death to the soul deceived by them. It was good for the people who grumbled against the Lord to be prostrated by the bites of serpents, for this outward scourge would make them realize how much inward damage they suffered because of their grumbling. The bronze serpent that was raised up so that those who were bitten might look at it and be healed represents our Redeemer in his passion on the cross, for the kingdom of death and sin is conquered only by faith in him.

The sins which drag both soul and body to destruction are well described as serpents, not only because they are fiery and poisonous and cunning enough to destroy us, but because a serpent persuaded our first parents, who were immortal, to commit the sin through which they became subject to death. Our Lord, who came in the likeness of sinful flesh, is rightly portrayed as the bronze serpent because as the bronze serpent was the same as the fiery serpents except that it contained no poisonous or hurtful fire, and when it was raised up it healed those bitten by serpents, so also the Redeemer of humankind clothed himself not in sinful flesh, but in the likeness of sinful flesh, in which, by suffering death on the cross, he delivered those who believe in him from all sin and even from death itself.

Therefore *as Moses lifted up the serpent in the wilderness, so must the Son of man be lifted up;* for as those who looked at the bronze serpent set up as a sign were for a time healed of the physical death and injury produced by the serpents' bites, so also those who look at the mystery of the Lord's passion, believing, confessing, and sincerely imitating him, are saved completely and for ever from the death of both soul and body which they had incurred through sin. Accordingly the text continues: *so that all who believe in him may not perish, but may have eternal life.* These words make it clear that whoever believes in Christ not only escapes the pain of punishment but also receives a life that is eternal. And here we see the difference between symbol and truth, for the one prolongs this temporal life, while the other gives a life that will be endless. We must make sure, however, that the truths our minds perceive are given fitting practical expression, so that by confessing the true faith, and living devout and disciplined lives, we may deserve to attain the fullness of the life which has no end.

*(Homily II, 18: CCL CXXII, 315-17)*

---

**Bede** (c. 673-735), who received the title of Venerable less than a century after his death, was placed at the age of seven in the monastery of Wearmouth, then ruled by Saint Benet Biscop. From there he was sent to Jarrow, probably at the time of its foundation in about 681. At the age of thirty he was ordained priest. His whole life was devoted to the study of Scripture, to teaching, writing, and the prayer of the Divine Office. He was famous for his learning, although he never went beyond the bounds of his native Northumbria. Bede is best known for his historical works, which earned him the title "Father of English History." His *Historia Ecclesiastica Gentis Anglorum* is a primary source for early English history, especially valuable because of the care he took to give his authorities, and to separate historical fact from hearsay and tradition. In 1899 Bede was proclaimed a doctor of the Church.

# All Saints

*Gospel:* Matthew 5:1-12

Be glad and rejoice, for your reward will be great in heaven.

*Commentary:* Augustine

*Blessed are the pure in heart, for they shall see God.* This is the end of our love, an end by which we are not consumed but perfected. Food is finished when it is eaten, a garment when it is woven. Both the one and the other have an end, but the end of the one is consumption; the end of the other is perfection.

Whatever we do now, whatever good deeds we perform, whatever we strive for, whatever praiseworthy object we long for, whatever we blamelessly desire, we shall need no more when we come to the vision of God. What is there to seek for when God is present? What will suffice if God does not?

We want to see God, we strive to see him, we long to see him. Who does not? But notice what scripture says: *Blessed are the pure in heart, for they shall see God.* Provide yourself with that by which you may see him; for, to give a physical example, what use would longing to see a sunrise be if you were half blind? If the eye is healthy that light will bring joy: if the eye is unhealthy that light will be a torment. You will not be permitted to see with an impure heart what can be seen only with a pure heart. Far from seeing you will be repelled, driven away.

*Blessed are the pure in heart, for they shall see God.* How often already has the Evangelist mentioned the blessed, the reason for their blessedness, their works, their services, their merits, their rewards! But nowhere does he say that *they shall see God. Blessed are the poor in spirit, for theirs is the kingdom of heaven. Blessed are the gentle, for they shall inherit the earth. Blessed are those who mourn, for they shall be comforted. Blessed are those who hunger and thirst for righteousness, for they shall be satisfied. Blessed are the merciful, for they shall obtain mercy.* Of none of these is it said that they shall see God. It is when we come to the pure in heart that the vision of God is promised. This is because it is the heart that has eyes capable of seeing God. To these eyes the apostle Paul refers when he says: *having the eyes of your hearts enlightened.*

At present, as becomes their infirmity, these eyes are enlightened by faith: hereafter, as will become their strength, they will be enlightened by sight. *As long as we are in the body, we are absent from the Lord, for we walk by faith and not by sight.* While we are in this state of faith, what is said of us? *Now we see in a mirror dimly, but then we shall see face to face.*

*(Sermon 53, 6: PL 38, 366)*

**Augustine** (354-430) was born at Thagaste in Africa and received a Christian education, although he was not baptized until 387. In 391 he was ordained priest and in 395 he became coadjutor bishop to Valerius of Hippo, whom he succeeded in 396. Augustine's theology was formulated in the course of his struggle with three heresies: Manichaeism, Donatism, and Pelagianism. His writings are voluminous and his influence on subsequent theology immense. He molded the thought of the Middle Ages down to the thirteenth century. Yet he was above all a pastor and a great spiritual writer.

# All Souls

*Gospel:* Matthew 5:1-12

Blessed are the poor in spirit, for theirs is the kingdom of heaven.

*Commentary:* Catherine of Genoa

The souls in purgatory cannot think,
"I am here, and justly so because of my sins,"
or "I wish I had never committed such sins
for now I would be in paradise. . . ."
Such is their joy in God's will, in his pleasure,
that they have no concern for themselves
but dwell only on their joy in God's ordinance. . . .
Only once do they understand
the reason for their purgatory:
the moment in which they leave this life.
After this moment, that knowledge disappears.
Immersed in charity, incapable of deviating from it,
they can only will or desire pure love.
There is no joy save that in paradise
to be compared with the joy of the souls in purgatory. . . .
Joy in God, oneness with him, is the end of these souls,
an instinct implanted in them at their creation. . . .
That is why the soul seeks to cast off
any and all impediments, so that it can be lifted up to God;
and such impediments
are the cause of the suffering of the souls in purgatory.
Not that the souls dwell on their suffering;
they dwell rather
on the resistance they feel in themselves
against the will of God,
against his intense and pure love bent on nothing

but drawing them up to him. . . .
The soul becomes like gold
that becomes purer as it is fired,
all dross being cast out.
The last stage of love
is that which does its work without human doing.
If humans were to be aware of the many hidden flaws in
them
they would despair.
These flaws are burned away in the last stage of love.
God then shows the soul its weakness,
so that the soul may see the workings of God.
If we are to become perfect,
the change must be brought about in us and without us;
that is, the change is to be the work not of human beings
but of God.
This, the last stage of love,
is the pure and intense love of God alone.
The overwhelming love of God
gives the soul a joy beyond words.
In purgatory great joy and great suffering
do not exclude one another.

*(Purgation and Purgatory, Classics of Western Spirituality,
71-72.76.78-79.81-82)*

---

**Catherine of Genoa** (1447-1510), a Fieschi by birth, was married at the age
of sixteen to Giuliano Adorno, a worldly-minded youth who did not care for
her. After ten unhappy years she was suddenly converted to ardent love of
God. Later her husband too was converted and helped her to care for the sick
in a hospital at Genoa. Her teachings, compiled by others, are contained in
*Purgation and Purgatory* and *The Spiritual Dialogue.*

# Dedication
## of the Lateran Basilica

*Gospel:* Luke 19:1-10

Today salvation has come to this house.

*Commentary:* Bernard

Today we celebrate another glorious feast: it is the feast of the
Lord's house, of God's temple, of the city of the eternal king, of
Christ's bride. Let us ask ourselves what this house of God, this
temple, this city, and this bride can be. With awe and reverence I say:
It is we ourselves. I say it is we ourselves, but in the heart of God; it
is we ourselves, but by his grace and not by any merits of our own.
We humans must beware of appropriating what belongs to God, of
taking the glory to ourselves; otherwise, if we exalt ourselves, he will
humble us and bring us down to our proper level. On the other hand,
a humble acknowledgement of our maladies will arouse his compassion. Indeed this is enough to make God feed us in our hunger like a
well-to-do father. So under his protection we shall have bread in
abundance and thus become his house in which life-giving food is
never lacking.

Bear in mind also that he describes his house as a house of prayer,
and that holiness befits this house; then the purity of self-restraint will
accompany the tears of repentance, and what is already God's house
will become his temple as well. *Be holy, says the Lord, because I am
holy.* And the Apostle says: *Do you not realize that your bodies are
the temple of the Holy Spirit and the Holy Spirit dwells in you?*

But is even holiness enough? According to the Apostle, peace too is
necessary, for he says: *Strive to be at peace with everyone, and to achieve
the holiness without which no one can see God.* It is peace that makes
brothers dwell together in unity and builds for our king, the true king of
peace, a new city also called Jerusalem, which means "vision of peace."

But how can so great a king become a bridegroom, and a city a bride? This is possible to love alone, which is as strong as death, and can do anything. Can it not easily lift her up, when it has already brought him down?

And so, if the abundance of our food shows us to be the house of a great Father, if holiness shows us to be God's temple, if the sharing of a common life shows us to be the city of the great king, and if love shows us to be the bride of the immortal bridegroom, then we can surely say without hesitation that today's feast is our feast. Nor should you be surprised that such a feast is celebrated here on earth; it is, after all, being celebrated in heaven too! For if as Truth says, so it must be true, there is joy in heaven and even among God's angels over a single sinner repenting, then the joy there today must be many times greater at so many sinners repenting. Let us then share the rejoicing of the angels, let us share the joy of God, and let us keep today's feast with thanksgiving, for the fact that it is our own should make us all the more willing to celebrate it.

*(Sermon 5 on the Dedication of a Church, 1.8-10:*
*PL 183, 529.534-35)*

**Bernard** (1090-1153) entered the monastery of Citeaux with thirty companions in 1112. He received his monastic training under the abbot, Saint Stephen Harding, who sent him in 1115 to make a foundation at Clairvaux in France. Soon one of the most influential religious forces in Europe, Bernard was instrumental in founding the Knights Templar and in the election of Pope Innocent I in 1130. He was a strenuous opponent of writers such as Abelard, Gilbert de la Porree, and Henry of Lausanne. Above all, Bernard was a monk; his sermons and theological writings show an intimate knowledge of Scripture, a fine eloquence, and an extraordinarily sublime mysticism.

# Immaculate Conception

*Gospel:* Luke 1:26-38

Rejoice, most favored one, the Lord is with you.

*Commentary:* John Henry Newman

Now, as you know, it has been held from the first, and defined from an early age, that Mary is the Mother of God. She is not merely the mother of our Lord's manhood, or of our Lord's body, but she is to be considered the mother of the Word himself, the Word incarnate. God, in the person of the Word, the Second Person of the all-glorious Trinity, took the substance of his human flesh from her, and clothed in it he lay within her; and he bore it about with him after birth, as a sort of badge and witness that he, though God, was hers. He was nursed and tended by her; he was suckled by her; he lay in her arms. As time went on, he ministered to her, and obeyed her. He lived with her for thirty years, in one house, with an uninterrupted intercourse, and with only the saintly Joseph to share it with him. She was the witness of his growth, of his joys, of his sorrows, of his prayers; she was blest with his smile, with the touch of his hand, with the whisper of his affection, with the expression of his thoughts and his feelings for that length of time. Now, my brethren, what ought she to be, what is it becoming that she should be, who was so favored?

Such a question was once asked by a heathen king, *What should be done to the man whom the king desires to honor?* And he received the following answer, *The man whom the king wishes to honor ought to be clad in the king's apparel, and to receive the royal diadem on his head; and let the first among the king's princes hold his horse.* So stands the case with Mary; she gave birth to the Creator, and what recompense shall be made her? What shall be done to her, who had this relationship to the Most High?

I answer: Nothing is too high for her to whom God owes his human life; no exuberance of grace, no excess of glory but is becoming, but is to be expected there, where God has lodged himself, whence God has issued. Let her *be clad in the king's apparel,* that is, let the fullness of the Godhead so flow into her that she may be a figure of the incommunicable sanctity, and beauty, and glory of God himself: that she may be the mirror of justice, the mystical rose, the tower of ivory, the house of gold, the morning star. Let her *receive the king's diadem upon her head,* as the queen of heaven, the mother of all the living, the health of the weak, the refuge of sinners, the comforter of the afflicted. And *let the first amongst the king's princes walk before her,* let angels, and prophets, and apostles, and martyrs, and all saints kiss the hem of her garment and rejoice under the shadow of her throne.

We should be prepared then, my brethren, to believe, that the Mother of God is full of grace and glory, from the very fitness of such a dispensation. St. John Baptist was sanctified by the Spirit before his birth; shall Mary be only equal to him? Is it not fitting that her privilege should surpass his? Is it wonderful, if grace, which anticipated his birth by three months, should in her case run up to the very first moment of her being, outstrip the imputation of sin, and be beforehand with the usurpation of Satan? Mary must surpass all the saints; the very fact that certain privileges are known to have been theirs persuades us, almost from the necessity of the case, that she had the same and higher. Her conception then was immaculate, in order that she might surpass all saints in the date as well as the fullness of her sanctification.

*(Discourses addressed to Mixed Congregations, 362-65.372)*

---

**Newman, John Henry** (1801-90) was born in London and brought up in the Church of England. He went up to Trinity College, Oxford in 1817, became a Fellow of Oriel five years later, was ordained deacon in 1824 and appointed Vicar of Saint Mary's, Oxford, in 1832. The impact of his sermons was tremendous. He was the leading spirit in the Tractarian Movement (1833-41) and the condemnation of *Tract 90* led to his resignation from Saint Mary's in 1843. Two years later he was received into the Catholic Church. He was ordained in Rome and founded a house of Oratorians in Birmingham. Newman's *Essay on the Development Christian Doctrine* throws light on his withdrawal of previous objections to Roman Catholicism; his *Apologia* reveals the deepest motives underlying his outward attitudes, and the *Grammar of Assent* clarifies the subjective content of commitment to faith. In 1879 he was made a cardinal and he died at Edgbaston in 1890.

# *Index of Scripture*

# Index of Authors